# Light Bright

# Light Bright

Joyce L. Martin

**An Activity-Centered Enrichment Program for Grades 2–6**

**PRUFROCK PRESS, INC.**
P.O. Box 8813
Waco, TX 76714-8813
Phone: (800) 998-2208
Fax: (800) 240-0333
http://www.prufrock.com

To bright, young children everywhere who love to explore new ideas, to create, and to challenge themselves. May the ideas presented in this book ever expand your knowledge, help you realize your potential, and reveal your special talents.

To teachers of the young gifted and talented who have the complex job of challenging bright minds and who desire to ignite those minds with the fervent passion to learn. May the enrichment curriculum presented here enhance your own ideas and activities for gifted education.

To parents who wish their children could have had the opportunity for a Light Bright experience. It's not too late—these ideas are only a beginning.

# Contents

# Figures & Worksheets

**Worksheets—Continued**

I would like to express my appreciation to the many people who helped me with the tremendous task of publishing the original version of this manual.

There are three to whom I am indebted forever. To Jack, my husband, for his support, advice, and patience. And, to Sean and Dawn, my bright children, for the spark that kindled the fire.

To Rena F. Subotnik, Ph.D., Hunter College–C.U.N.Y, for encouragement and wisdom and for providing a challenge that was beyond my greatest dreams.

To Joseph S. Renzulli, director of the National Research Center on the Gifted and Talented, for sharing his phenomenal wealth of knowledge of the gifted and talented, for his foresight in addressing their special educational needs, for his inspiration to all who teach them, and to his long-standing dedication to talented youth all over the world!

To Barbara, for her creative artwork and for being my mentor on self-publishing.

To colleague Carolyn Brooke who contributed substantially to the development of Light Bright.

To the staff, especially the second-grade teachers, parents, and volunteers at Helen Haller Elementary School for their enthusiasm, support, and contributions.

Special thanks go to the Light Bright children at Helen Haller who, because of their eagerness, creativity, and love of learning, kept the program growing and evolving.

My heartfelt thanks goes to these people and to the many others who directly or indirectly contributed to the development of this program.

> *To be what we are, and to become what we are capable of becoming, is the only end of life.*
> —Robert Louis Stevenson

Fellow Teachers:

Have you ever wondered what to do with Brian, a student who quickly absorbs and accurately completes all the work you give him? He's constantly at your desk asking, "What can I do now?" Do you give him another worksheet? Do you tell him to read a book or ask him to help others with their assignments? How often have you found yourself without the time or resources to devote to the Brians of your classroom?

You sense that Brian is academically gifted. You review his file and find that he has received high scores on standardized tests and good marks on his report cards. You know that he is extremely interested in insects, but you just don't have the time to help him pursue his interest. There is no gifted program in your school or, if there is, it may be limited and restrictive. Multiply Brian by 10 students and it's enough to make teachers gray before their time.

In 1987, this was the situation in which my colleague, Carolyn Brooke, and I found ourselves. We sat down one day after school, closed the door, and talked for hours. It was behind those closed doors that Light Bright was born. Incidentally, I'm convinced that the greatest ideas come out of teacher brainstorming sessions that take place behind closed classroom doors. Unfortunately, many of these ideas are never shared nor implemented.

Are you a classroom teacher frustrated because your school does not provide educational opportunities for highly capable students? Light Bright used as an enrichment center for regular classrooms in grades 2–6, can be an alternative for gifted education especially if your school district has limited dollars for gifted programs. The center is adaptable to any elementary school population and configuration. It can be located in a pod, a hallway, a spare classroom, or in a corner of a classroom.

Are you a librarian or a part-time specialist who suddenly has been asked to provide gifted education for the school's top students? Do you have training in teaching gifted students? Light Bright used as the Pull-Out Model offers you the opportunity to implement an inexpensive gifted program for the elementary grades in your school. You need not spend the summer taking college courses in gifted education, although such classes would be beneficial.

Are you a gifted specialist in the elementary grades who receives an abundance of mail offering this and that program, but the materials and implementation plan are so expensive that it does not

fit within your budget? The low cost of implementing Light Bright will make you want to investigate further. And, if you are lucky enough to have a wealth of gifted materials already, Light Bright provides a way to organize these materials into a sequential plan for a total gifted program.

Light Bright is an independent learning center that is learner-motivated, self-directed, and self-paced. The program provides hands-on activities that foster creativity, originality, and higher level thinking skills. Children have the opportunity for in-depth exploration of hobbies, talents, and interests. Students use new techniques, materials, and forms; improve their research methods and independent study skills; and develop problem-solving techniques as they make creations.

Used as the Classroom Model, Light Bright is not exclusive. It can motivate the slow learner or lazy student and provide an opportunity for every student to participate in challenging activities. The ideas presented in this manual are ones that have been field-tested—they are ideas that work!

An outstanding feature of the program is that it involves parents, community resources, and volunteers. As a classroom teacher, I certainly don't pretend that I know everything about every subject. I welcome the expertise of individuals who have more knowledge in their field than I ever could have in my lifetime. I have found that their creativity in presenting their materials to children is much more exciting than the lessons I teach on subjects with which I've had no training or personal experience.

The Light Bright manual has been divided into three phases:

- **Phase I–Exploratory Baskets;**
- **Phase II–Creative Teaching; and**
- **Phase III–Community Resources and Mentors.**

Each part of the program builds upon skills presented in the previous phase and provides opportunities for further in-depth exploration.

Basket Exploration begins with larger groups of students exploring a variety of subjects and topics. Creative Teaching provides opportunities for small groups of children to examine a subject in greater depth and detail. The program concludes with Community Resources and Mentors, which offers a student the chance to pair with a mentor for intensified study of a subject and provides opportunities for the student to visit occupational sites.

Part one of the manual presents the mechanics of Phase I–Exploratory Baskets, including the organization of volunteers, the selection of location and space, the establishment of student expectations and requirements, and recommendations for time management. Phase I includes additional resources for enrichment basket preparation and suggested basket activities that have worked in the past.

Basket exploration provides students the opportunity to explore new materials in their unique way. This first phase consists of 20 or 30 baskets containing noncurriculum enrichment or gifted materials from various academic and creative areas. This arrangement permits children to clarify their own interests. Baskets are self-directed and contain all materials necessary for children to create a product directly related to their learning experience.

The baskets can be color coded and range in complexity and thinking skills according to ~~~om's Taxonomy. A computer may also be added to the center. Directions for setting up Kids ~~~hing Day and ways children can share their Light Bright creations are included.

Part one concludes with recommended resources for basket contents and lesson plans for suggested basket activities that have been popular at our Light Bright Center. The materials are from the areas of art, crafts, mathematics, science, writing and poetry, and reading. Ideas offered for games, research projects, and inventions allow children to create something new—it's their chance to become inventors.

Part two is comprised of the organization and suggested activities for Phase II–Creative Teaching, which occurs at the Light Bright Center. Part two does not include the baskets. During this phase, parents and community members share an interest, skill, hobby, or talent with a small group of children with similar interests. The teachers of the lessons are free to teach content as they see fit using their own materials and resources, as well as materials from the school.

These small-group activities help children work more effectively with content. Sample lessons from art, computers, drama, food and nutrition, foreign languages, music, reading, science, and writing are included.

Part three will give you ideas for possible mentorship activities used in Phase III–Community Resources and Mentors. This phase uses parents and community persons to provide mentorship teaching by working with one or two students who have been identified as highly talented in a specific area such as mathematics, art, computers, and so forth. This chance to interact with experts and to work in real-life situations is invaluable.

At this level, students can explore subjects of interest in greater depth than is possible in the classroom or even in small groups. You will find sample activities and ideas for mentorships from professional occupations and trades and from specific subject areas such as mathematics, computers, electronics, and marine biology. This phase includes ideas for field trips to occupational sites.

Light Bright is not an officially validated program, nor has it been sanctioned by superiors, nor written by professors with doctoral degrees. It was created by teachers for children because we felt the tremendous need to provide young gifted and talented children with opportunities to pursue, reach, and explore their potential. It was this desire coupled with the children's enthusiasm that kept the program going and evolving into the total program presented in this manual.

The beauty of the classroom model is that the classroom teacher is still in control. The teacher determines which students will go to Light Bright. It is not a pull-out program for any student. The underachiever, the slow student, or the unidentified gifted child has the same opportunity to go to Light Bright that the gifted student has. The teachers determine when Light Bright is open and where it is located. Used as the regular gifted program, Light Bright provides a total program to be

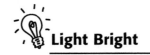 

used with grades 2–6. Light Bright was designed with flexibility in mind, so schools can easily tailor it to fit within their curriculum.

Light Bright provides an opportunity for the highest level of individualized instruction as the learner directs his or her own learning activities. Lifelong learning will be the way of life for most gifted and talented students and Light Bright provides a learning resource to facilitate their learning. Treffinger has presented the Self-Directed Learning Model (Treffinger, 1975) for helping to move learning from teacher-directed and controlled to learning-directed.

According to Treffinger's model, self-directed learning is an organized, structured strategy for giving children opportunities to gain skills and abilities in their areas of special interest. The teacher—who serves as a resource and guide when needed, helping to establish topics, goals, and procedures—is part of the project, but not its director. Learners receive less direction as they become more self-directed. I am confident that your Light Bright Center will provide your gifted and talented students with this exceptional educational experience.

Since the inception of the Light Bright program in 1987 and the publication of the original *Light Bright* teacher's manual in 1989, many educators in the U.S. and Canada have implemented the program in their schools. The consistent feedback from teachers using this enrichment model is how closely it resembles Dr. Joseph Renzulli's Enrichment Triad Model (Renzulli, 1977). In the beginning, Light Bright was not intended to parallel the Renzulli model. However, as Light Bright developed, it just naturally evolved into the model presented in this manual, giving exemplary educational merit to the Renzulli paradigm created more than 20 years ago.

After reviewing a copy of this book, Renzulli stated, "I must say that I thoroughly enjoyed reviewing your book and couldn't help but think how wonderful it would be if all elementary students had the opportunity to engage in these kinds of exciting activities."

Certainly our premise on how to educate children in today's schools is the same in that we as educators are both programmatically and educationally obligated to do all that we can do to make schools better places for all learners. As many of us have discovered, curriculum originally developed solely for the gifted and talented can benefit all students and contribute to total school improvement.

# What is Schoolwide Enrichment?

Schoolwide enrichment is a systematic set of specific strategies for increasing student effort, enjoyment, and performance, and for integrating a broad range of advanced level learning experiences and higher order thinking skills into any curricular area or course of study (Renzulli & Reis, 1985). This research-supported plan, developed by Joseph Renzulli and Sally Reis, is designed for general education, but is based on a large number of instructional methods and curricular practices that had their origins in special programs for high-ability students. The Light Bright program is a schoolwide enrichment model for grades 2–6 that provides a detailed plan or blueprint for total school improvement; however, each school develops its own unique program based on local resources, student populations, school leadership dynamics, faculty strengths, and creativity.

## Goals of Schoolwide Enrichment

- To develop the talent potentials of young people by systematically assessing strengths, providing enrichment opportunities, resources, and services to develop strengths of all students and using a flexible approach to curricular differentiation and the use of school time.

- To improve the academic performance of all students in all areas of the regular curriculum and to blend into the standard curriculum activities that will engage students in meaningful and enjoyable learning.

- To create a learning community that honors ethnic, gender, and cultural diversity, mutual respect, and caring attitudes toward one another, respect for democratic principles, and preservation of the Earth's resources.

- To implement a democratic school governance procedure that includes appropriate decision-making opportunities for students, parents, teachers, and administrators (Renzulli & Reis, 1985).

## The Program Includes:

- High standards and advanced levels of academic challenge for all students.

- The traditional remedial method of instruction is replaced with interest-based enrichment and open-ended learning experiences.

- Motivation, creativity, thinking skills, and cooperativeness are developed by taking student learning styles, talents, and interests into consideration.

- The hands-on approach to enrichment focuses on the student's role as a first-hand inquirer, the teacher being the facilitator of the learning experience, not the director.

# Phase I–Exploratory Baskets
# A Time to Investigate and Create

# Chapter 1: Getting Ready

Light Bright volunteers are the backbone of the program. Without them, a great demand would be placed on the teachers. In the beginning, as with any new program, teachers will have to put in time. With thorough volunteer training and organization, Light Bright will eventually become an independent center with little demand on the classroom teacher. Gifted teachers will welcome the expertise of volunteers in subject areas where they may have insufficient knowledge. Light Bright provides an invaluable opportunity for children and adults to work together in a nurturing and learning environment. Ideas for soliciting, training, and organizing volunteers are discussed in this chapter.

Time management, student accountability, record keeping, discipline, location and space, and teacher time are discussed in this chapter. Since most gifted programs will have established criteria for determining how and when the students go to the gifted resource room, student accountability, record keeping, and so forth, the emphasis of this chapter is on the Classroom Model. However, if you are a teacher new to the gifted program or are establishing a gifted program, you may want to adopt some of the procedures in this chapter.

> Some men see things as they
> are and say 'why'?
> I dream things that never were
> and say 'why not'?
>
> —George Bernard Shaw

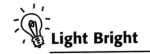 

## Organizing Volunteers

Light Bright basket activities are facilitated by volunteer moms, dads, aides, or resource persons from the community. At the beginning of the school year, a volunteer letter is sent home to all of the parents of children in grades 2–6, to community service groups, as well as hobby groups. A sample letter and survey follow.

After the surveys have been returned to school, teachers in grades 2–6 or the gifted teacher(s) organize the Parent/Community Interest Surveys according to interests and skills. This becomes your master list. The next step is to divide the list of volunteers into three groups according to whether they will be volunteers in Phase I, Phase II, or Phase III.

For example, some volunteers will want to help with the program, but feel that they do not have a talent or interest to share. These volunteers are good candidates to assist with Phase I–Exploratory Baskets. Other volunteers will be very excited to share a skill, talent, or interest with a small group of children and even have their own ideas and materials. They are great teachers for Phase II–Creative Teaching. There will be some volunteers who do not feel comfortable with children, but who do have a skill or trade to share. These people will make great mentors for Phase III–Community Resources and Mentorship as they will be working with only one or two students.

Now that you have a master list, you will need to select one person to be the volunteer coordinator. This person will be in charge of contacting volunteers, arranging on-site occupational visits and transportation, and scheduling volunteers for all three phases. Once a schedule is arranged, it is posted at the Light Bright Center and updated weekly.

Finally, you will need to call a volunteer meeting when as many volunteers as possible are available. One teacher may be in charge of this meeting or all of the teachers may be involved. The mechanics of the program are explained, schedules are verified, a starting date is established, and Light Bright volunteers tour the center. Discuss your school's discipline policy at this time. A question-and-answer session concludes the meeting. A typical Volunteer Training Agenda for the meeting follows.

Volunteers are in charge of keeping baskets full of materials. You may need to train your volunteers to use the computer, copier, and so forth, and inform them where additional supplies are located. They are also in charge of filing students' unfinished work and Light Bright materials. A filing cabinet is a must. A list of volunteer responsibilities follows.

Teachers have found it easier to begin their Light Bright Center with only Phase I–Exploratory Baskets. Basket preparation takes the most teacher time, unlike Creative Teaching or Mentorship where the major responsibility of preparation falls onto the volunteers. This arrangement will also give you and your volunteers some time to get a feeling of the program and iron out the wrinkles. When you feel the center is running smoothly, you may begin preparing for Phase II and Phase III.

# Volunteer Training Agenda

I.   Background information on the Light Bright program—what it is and how it works, with emphasis on Phase I–Exploratory Baskets

    A. Share the *Light Bright* Teacher's Manual

II.  Inventory of the Light Bright Center

    A. Tour the Center

III. Procedures

    A. Light Bulbs

    B. Light Bright Messages

    C. Volunteer Responsibilities

    D. Rules

    E. Unfinished Work

    F. Discipline Policy

IV.  The Basket Center

    A. Note Cards

    B. Materials

    C. Supplies

    D. Evaluation Procedures

V.   Select Light Bright Coordinator

VI.  Schedules

VII. Questions

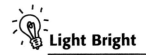 

# Volunteer Responsibilities

1. Assist students in selecting and checking out a basket.

2. Explain directions and extensions on the white and blue note cards in the basket. Remind students that they must complete the white note card first.

3. Check to see that all necessary supplies and materials are in each basket when it is checked out and when it is returned.

4. Maintain a list of needed basket items that have been depleted and are not available at the Light Bright Center.

5. Make sure that the Light Bright Messages are completed for each student and that there is a supply of the messages at the center.

6. Answer questions and assist students when necessary in planning, completing, and editing project completion.

7. Store unfinished projects with Light Bright Messages at the center.

# Light Bright

To interested parents and community members:

An important aspect of educating our children is providing these young people with challenging experiences. A wide variety of assistance is needed this year for our Light Bright program, a hands-on enrichment center for our students in grades 2–6. I hope to draw more effectively on some of the resources in our own community. I would like to provide more opportunities for these young people for a wide exposure to people and ideas and a chance for some in-depth exploration.

I hope that you will be able to share your profession or trade and interest areas with groups of students. I would especially like to identify some persons who would be willing to explore a common interest with one or two students over a period of time. This could be a chance for you to deal intensively with a topic that intrigues you and to help a student learn some valuable "real-world" skills to which he or she might not be exposed in the regular school curriculum.

Filling out the survey does not, of course, indicate that you are making a firm commitment. After reviewing your responses, I will follow through with further contact. The survey will give me some helpful information about you and your talents—and might give you some surprising insights into the potential value of your profession and interests.

Thank you for your interest and time.

Sincerely,

# Parent/Community Member Interest Survey

Student:_____   Teacher:_____

## Professions and/or Trades
(Check appropriate areas.)

- ❏ Actor
- ❏ Architect
- ❏ Attorney
- ❏ Banker
- ❏ Computer Specialist*
- ❏ Dentist
- ❏ Doctor (general)
- ❏ Doctor (specialist)
- ❏ Educator
- ❏ Electrician
- ❏ Engineer
- ❏ Journalist
- ❏ Marketing
- ❏ Mechanic
- ❏ Taxidermist
- ❏ Veterinarian
- ❏ Other*

\*   Please Specify _____
_____

## Interest Areas
(Check appropriate areas.)

- ❏ Coins
- ❏ Computers*
- ❏ Crafts*
- ❏ Dance
- ❏ Drama
- ❏ Gardening
- ❏ Painting
- ❏ Photography
- ❏ Politics
- ❏ Puppetry
- ❏ Sculpture
- ❏ Stamps
- ❏ Stock Market
- ❏ Travel
- ❏ Weather
- ❏ Writing
- ❏ Other*

\*   Please Specify _____
_____

Other ways you might be willing to assist with the program: _____
_____
_____

Name: _____   Phone:_____
Address:_____   E-mail Address: _____

### Preferences
Day of Week: _____   Time: _____
Area of Speciality:_____

Please return to school by: _____

Thank you for your support of Light Bright.

## Time Management

### Classroom Model

Certain limitations need to be enforced to allow every child a Light Bright basket experience. For most students, 20–30 minutes is sufficient time to complete the white note card activity in the basket. When the student progresses to the more difficult blue note card activities in the basket, the project could take weeks to complete. The projects can either be taken back to the classroom to be completed or stored at the center for future work. Make sure that the Light Bright Message stays with the project until completion. However, if a child is very excited about what he or she is doing, instruct the volunteers to continue letting the child work if at all possible. After all, the purpose of Light Bright is to turn on the "light bulb."

The best time for Light Bright to be open for grades 2–6 is the last hour of the morning before lunch and the last hour of the school day. Other times interfere with daily tasks, directions, and instructions. By the end of the morning, your more capable students will be done with their work and will want something to do.

The morning hour seems most appropriate for Phase I–Exploratory Baskets and the afternoon hour for Phase II–Creative Teaching and/or Phase III–Community Resources and Mentorship. Basket exploration requires more active participation and provides an outlet for restlessness that usually occurs at the end of the morning. Likewise, a different teacher, which is an essential component of Creative Teaching and Mentorship, is refreshing at the end of the day. Gifted children will usually understand concepts and learn skills quicker than other children. Time spent learning at Light Bright, rather than in the regular classroom, need not be made up.

It is highly recommended that the Light Bright Basket Center be open every day of the week. This is to ensure time for every student in grades 2–6 to experience basket exploration, to ensure repetitive experiences for the highly capable, and to ensure continuity for students working on long-term projects. Experience has shown that students can lose interest in their creations if they have to wait days to continue.

Creative teachers (Phase II) and mentors (Phase III) may not always be available on weekdays in the afternoon. Whenever a resource person from your community volunteers his or her valuable time and expertise, make every effort to adjust your schedule to accommodate him or her.

### Pull-Out Model

If you are the gifted teacher, you could actually have all three phases occurring at the same time in your classroom, with one group of children exploring the baskets, one group in a Creative Teaching session and a few students working with mentors or with you. Of course, this depends on available space. Another option is to have certain hours of the day only open for basket exploration, for small-group teaching, and for mentorship.

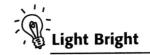 

### Light Bright Light Bulbs

When a child goes to the Light Bright Center, he or she puts a paper light bulb on his or her desk. This indicates to the teacher and the other students that the child is at Light Bright. If there are no light bulbs left hanging, this indicates to students that Light Bright is full and they must wait until a light bulb is returned in order to go to the center.

To make a light bulb, photocopy Figure 1 onto yellow tagboard, laminate, punch a hole, and loop with yellow yarn for convenient hanging in the classroom. The number of light bulbs you make depends on the number of children who can be managed at the center at a given time. When a child returns to class, he or she simply returns the light bulb to its central location. This is an indication that another child may go to the center.

**Figure 1: Light Bright Light Bulb**

# Light Bright Messages

Date: _____

Student: _____

Teacher: _____

Teacher Suggested Basket: _____

Basket Title: _____

What was accomplished? _____

_____

_____

Did the student enjoy the basket?

❑ Yes ❑ No

Any discipline problems? (explain) _____

_____

_____

Arrival Time: _____ Departure Time: _____

Volunteer: _____

Was objective/concept:

❑ Mastered

❑ Almost Mastered

❑ Not Mastered

**Figure 2: Light Bright Messages**

## Light Bright Messages

Once at Light Bright, the student must help the volunteer fill out the information on the Light Bright Messages (Figure 2). This is for your record keeping. The child is free to choose the basket he or she wishes to work on, but is held accountable for a constructive learning experience. The volunteer writes down the student's name and the chosen activity. When the student completes the project, the volunteer provides feedback to the student, writes a brief description of the activity performed, and evaluates whether the student mastered, almost mastered, or did not master the objective or concept.

Each lesson plan for basket activities (Chapter 5) provides a list of skills that are intended for assessing whether or not the student has mastered the concept or objective of the basket activity. One can assume that, if a student has created a satisfactory product from the basket, he or she has mastered the concept or objective. If a basket product is not acceptable and/or the student did not demonstrate understanding of the majority of the skills listed, then one can assume that the student did not master the concept or objective and may need to try it again. Keep in mind that the volunteers are making this assessment, and you may need to discuss evaluation procedures with them during the initial volunteer meeting. Volunteers will need to have access to a Light Bright manual during the time the center is open so that lesson plans are readily available.

Space is included for comments about any discipline problems that may have occurred. The rule is that any student who accumulates two reports of inappropriate behavior while at Light Bright will not be allowed back for two weeks. A third occurrence eliminates the student for one month. From past experience, a student seldom incurs more than one report of a discipline problem.

A separate Discipline Referral form follows on which the student must write down what he or she did wrong, then it must be signed by the volunteer. It is very important for the classroom teacher to follow-up on disciplinary action. Most volunteers are not equipped to deal with discipline. Furthermore, it is not their duty to do so. Light Bright is not a place to get rid of problem children; it is a learning place. Following through with expelling a child from the Light Bright Center for two weeks or a month will ensure the program's success.

As the classroom teacher, you may know that a student is particularly interested or gifted in a subject area or may have been excited about a lesson taught in class. There is space on Light Bright Messages for teacher suggestions. A note about a student's special interest provides an opportunity to let the child explore this interest further.

After the volunteer has signed the Light Bright Messages, the student brings it back to the classroom. There is a special basket for forms next to the hanging light bulbs placed in each classroom.

At the end of the day, the teacher reviews the forms, takes notes of any discipline problems, and files them in the individual student folders or portfolios. These are great records for parent-teacher conferences and written evidence that the school is providing opportunities to meet the needs of the highly capable child. At the end of each quarter, the Light Bright Messages can be sent home with the child's report card. Teachers may opt to send them home with the student's completed project.

# Discipline Referral

**Date:** _____     **Time:** _____

**Student:** _____     **Teacher:** _____

What did I do? _____

_____

_____

_____

_____

_____

**Light Bright Volunteer:** _____

- - - - - - - - - - - - - - - - - - - - - - - - - - - - - - - - - - - - - - - - - - - - - - - -

# Discipline Referral

**Date:** _____     **Time:** _____

**Student:** _____     **Teacher:** _____

What did I do? _____

_____

_____

_____

_____

_____

**Light Bright Volunteer:** _____

## Location and Space

Where you put your Light Bright Center depends on your student population, your school configuration, and the available space. A center could fit nicely into a central location, for example, a pod-like area between classrooms. A corner in a classroom, a portion of a hallway, or a spare classroom would do, as well.

You may choose to have a Light Bright Center at each grade (2–6) or have a central Light Bright Center for all grades depending on the configuration of your school. Whether you have one or five Light Bright Centers, the mechanics are the same.

You will need an area that includes space for 8' long x 3' high shelving, a desk for volunteers, a file cabinet for storing materials, and storage space for baskets. Depending on how many classes you have, you need floor space for 6–12 students to work. You could add a desk and a computer for student use.

Tables and chairs are nice, but not necessary. You can use lap boards as tables. Students can use the floor as a table. In fact, children rather like the idea of sprawling out on the floor. A carpet store could donate carpet samples for students to sit on. A bulletin board is nice to show off students' work.

Perhaps one of your teachers or parents enjoys carpentry as a hobby. These people would be good candidates to ask to build your shelving. Another possibility is to have the woodshop classes in your school district build the shelving for you. Any kind of shelving will do as long as it holds from 20–30 (12" x 14") baskets or tubs. You might even consider boards and bricks for shelving. Figures 3–5 are diagrams of possible locations for a Light Bright Center.

## Crunched for Space?

If you are fortunate enough to have gifted/enrichment teachers who travel to schools, Light Bright baskets can be stored on wheeled carts and rotated to classrooms during the designated time for student check out. The gifted/enrichment teacher works with students on the Light Bright projects in the classroom. If you do not have such specialists, a volunteer could administer the Light Bright baskets in the same manner, with volunteers assisting the students. Or, the classroom teacher may elect to do the Light Bright baskets on the cart with individual students or the entire class.

Light Bright activities can be housed in the library, a resource room, or in individual classrooms. The students check out the kits much like checking out a library book and work on them in the classroom. Ideas for storing the materials include large baggies, shoe boxes, pizza boxes, copy paper boxes, large manila envelopes, paper grocery bags, and large plastic ice cream containers from the ice cream shop. Research stores in your community. Most are willing to donate items to schools. Extra strong plastic media bags can be ordered from the Highsmith Company (see Chapter 4 for ordering information).

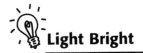 

## Possible Locations for Light Bright Center

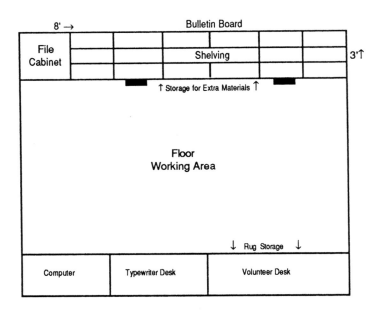

**Figure 3: Central Location or Spare Classroom**

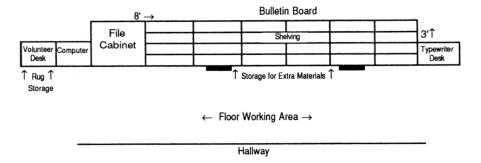

**Figure 4: Hallway Location**

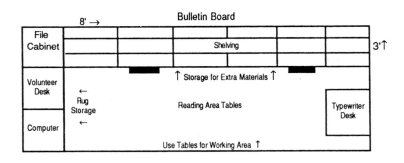

**Figure 5: Classroom Location**

## Teacher Time

It may appear that it takes a lot of time to review students' work before they are allowed to go to Light Bright. However, it is a task that becomes quite routine and should only take a few minutes a day. It doesn't take long to know who your capable students are, and it usually just takes a glance at the student's paper to see if it is accurate. Or, if you know students have tried very hard on an assignment because they want to go to Light Bright, by all means reward their efforts by letting them go to the center.

Because the Light Bright Center is open the last hour of the morning, many teachers will be in reading groups and will not want to be interrupted. Simply write the following on 3" x 5" note cards, laminate the cards, and take them with you to reading groups:

1) Redo—not correct.
2) See me after reading group.
3) Go to Light Bright Center.

When a child approaches you while you are in a reading group, show the appropriate card to the child and the child either has to go back and redo the work, or he or she can go to the Light Bright Center. You rarely have to say a word after the children adjust to the routine, and the reading group loses only seconds of your time.

If readers are grouped according to ability, you will probably find that most of your highly capable students are in your highest reading group. It is best to coordinate this reading group so that it is finished with reading by the time Light Bright is open in the morning so that they will be free to go. This plan also allows the classroom teacher to work on basic skills and review with the rest of the children in the classroom.

Reading group blocks allow valuable time to be spent with your students. Because they are grouped according to ability, you have an opportunity to use your own teaching strategies with your gifted students, assuming that they are in the same reading group. From past experience, this reading group usually finishes the required reading program halfway through the year. Rather than pushing them ahead to the next year's readers, use the remainder of the year's reading block time to do enrichment activities. This could include individualized projects or group projects. Light Bright is not designed to take away precious teacher-student time together. (See page 90–91 in the manual for 32 ways to share a book.)

In the beginning, as with any new program, all teachers wanting a Light Bright Center will have to put in time gathering materials, preparing baskets, organizing procedures and volunteers, and adapting to the program. But, the educational opportunities offered to children in such a center are well worth the time and effort.

# Chapter 2: Who Should Go to Light Bright?

Although Light Bright was created to meet the unique needs of the gifted and talented, other children should not be excluded from the center used as the Classroom Model. Many antigifted groups have formed based on the fact that gifted programs promote an "elite" group. Since Light Bright becomes very popular quickly, it would be quite unfair to let some students go and not allow others. This chapter will discuss Light Bright's unique plan to include all children while still providing multiple experiences for the gifted child.

As a classroom teacher, you will note that some highly capable children virtually identify themselves. Gifted children produce accurate, although not always neat, daily work, grasp fundamentals and concepts quickly, show interest in complex topics, and use vocabulary advanced for their age. This chapter will discuss the needs and characteristics, as well as two current definitions, of gifted and talented children. This information will help the classroom teacher identify gifted pupils without formally testing them.

Light Bright Student Expectations and Requirements are enclosed to serve as a guide in establishing your own expectations and requirements. You may choose to use the ones included or modify them to fit your needs.

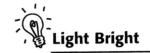 

## Definition of the Gifted and Talented

There are currently two definitions for the gifted and talented that are widely accepted by educators. The more popular definition is that of the United States Department of Education (U.S. 1993):

> Children and youth with outstanding talent perform or show the potential for performing at remarkably high levels of accomplishment when compared with others of their age, experience, or environment. These children and youth exhibit high performance and capability in intellectual creative, and/or artistic areas, possess an unusual leadership capacity, or excel in specific academic fields. They require services or activities not ordinarily provided by the school. Outstanding talents are present in children and youth from all cultural groups, across all economic strata, and in all areas of human endeavor. (p. 3)

The other frequently used definition is Dr. Joseph Renzulli's "three ring" definition:

> Giftedness consists of an interaction among three basic clusters of human traits—above average general abilities, high levels of task commitment, and high levels of creativity. Gifted and talented children are those possessing or capable of developing this composite set of traits and applying them to any potentially valuable area of human performance. Children who manifest or are capable of developing an interaction among these three clusters require a wide variety of educational opportunities and services that are not ordinarily provided through regular instructional programs. (Renzulli, 1978 p. 184)

Either definition is a move beyond the concept that giftedness is a high IQ score. Both definitions emphasize the need for "experiences" not ordinarily provided by the schools. Both stress achievement or the potential to achieve. The important fact here is that gifted children require educational opportunities beyond the curricula and instructional practices of regular education. Light Bright is a program that offers children these invaluable opportunities.

## Needs of the Gifted and Talented

Light Bright was created to meet the needs of gifted and talented students, as well as provide enrichment for all students. Some of their more obvious needs, as demonstrated by students who have participated in Light Bright experiences, include: learning activities at appropriate level and pace; experience in creative thinking and problem solving, especially in logical deduction and convergent problem solving; motivation to pursue higher goals; support of independence and self-direction; and freedom to express new ideas and opinions. All children need exposure to a variety of fields of study, professions, and occupations to uncover hidden talents. Access to a large supply of information about diverse topics, as is provided in the Light Bright baskets, reveals interests and potential abilities in students of all ages and backgrounds.

## Characteristics of the Gifted and Talented

Numerous books and articles have been written about the identification and typical characteristics of the gifted and talented. Some are extensive. Some have been debated. The Light Bright premise is that most teachers have an intuitive ability to recognize their highly capable students. One can readily observe when a student has mastered the regular curriculum quickly and accurately, finishes assignments, and seems restless and bored. And you don't have to be a specially trained teacher to know when a child has a high interest or special talent in a certain area.

Students who participate in Light Bright activities on a regular schedule consistently demonstrate the characteristics listed on the following page.

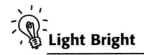 

| Characteristics of Gifted | Light Bright Program |
|---|---|
| • Is extremely curious.<br>• Wants to know the "how" and why."<br>• Has a wide variety of interests and hobbies. | Exposure to and exploration of a wide variety of topics and career exploration. |
| • Works independently.<br>• Is self-motivated.<br>• Reads, reads, reads.<br>• Prefers advanced reading. | Provision for exploring self-selected topics, independent study, and research. |
| • Masters the regular curriculum quickly and accurately.<br>• Grasps advanced concepts easily.<br>• Appears restless and bored.<br>• Is extremely energetic and driven. | Inclusion in curriculum of Bloom's higher level thinking skills (analysis, synthesis, and evaluation). |
| • Is creative and innovative.<br>• Develops original ideas and products.<br>• Presents new ways to solve problems.<br>• Is not afraid to try something new. | Provides outlet for creative/intellectual energy.<br>Allowance for differing ideas and opinions, originality. |
| • Dominates classroom discussions.<br>• Challenges textbook and teacher.<br>• Is labeled "bossy" by peers. | Provision to demonstrate leadership abilities. |
| • Is unusually sensitive.<br>• Is extremely self-critical.<br>• Is stubborn.<br>• Is a perfectionist. | Inclusion of activities to develop self-evaluation and establish values.<br>Less emphasis on end product, more emphasis on process. |

## Student Expectations and Requirements

Every student who goes to the Light Bright Center must fulfill the following expectations and requirements.

1.  Student has mastered educational objectives of daily work as demonstrated by accuracy. (Accuracy is defined as errorless. However, it is the teacher's discretion to determine how "errorless" a student's work must be before deciding whether or not he or she has mastered the concept behind the work.)
2.  Student can demonstrate independent study skills.
3.  Student is in control of behavior.
4.  Any student with two Light Bright misbehavior reports cannot return for two weeks.
5.  Any student with three Light Bright misbehavior reports cannot return for one month.
6.  Students must share their Light Bright creation in some way as indicated on the blue or white note cards in the baskets.
7.  All Light Bright volunteers are treated with respect and courtesy.
8.  All students must have teacher's permission to go to Light Bright.

The above expectations and requirements can be written and posted at the Light Bright Center.

Coordinators of gifted programs may have their own requirements and expectations for student participation in their programs. If not, the Classroom Model Student Expectations and Requirements can be modified to fit the needs of the gifted program.

At the beginning of the school year, expectations and requirements are reviewed with the children and posted on a large chart next to the light bulbs in each classroom. Younger children may not be able to read them, but they serve as a reminder of class discussion. Review them weekly the first month, once every two weeks the second month, and monthly thereafter. They will get the message that the Light Bright Center is a place that requires their best behavior.

Based on the assumption that your highly capable students master basic concepts and curricula quickly, they will not need to spend time on repetitive work. This allows them "free time" for visiting the center regularly. There may be times when a gifted student is having difficulty understanding a concept or skill. That student should stay in the classroom for reinforcement of the concept or skill to be mastered, thus allowing an opportunity for another student to go to Light Bright. This arrangement also allows the unidentified gifted student to frequent the center, whereas, in a formal gifted program, this student might not qualify.

Other students may visit the center once a week or even once a month. The number of times a student goes to Light Bright does not seem important as long as each has a Light Bright experience at some time. If there is a complaint, review the Light Bright expectations with the student. He or she may discover that one or more of the requirements have not been fulfilled.

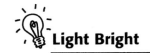 

Light Bright serves to motivate the student who has a hard time completing tasks and underachievers who try hard to master assignments so they may go to the Light Bright Center at the end of the morning. Although their work may not be of the same quality as the more able student, their efforts are rewarded by the Light Bright experience.

Identification of the gifted and talented is demanding, difficult, and time consuming. Some children virtually identify themselves, while others defy well-guided identification procedures. The advantage of establishing a Light Bright Center is that all children, whether they've been formally identified or not, have the opportunity to pursue an interest, explore new ideas, and think at higher levels. Test scores can be of great value in determining which students go into a gifted program, but children need no formal test scores in order to participate when Light Bright is used as an enrichment center.

# Chapter 3:
# The Basket Center

Now that you have volunteers organized, light bulbs made, Light Bright Messages copied, a place for your center established, and basket shelving intact, you need to purchase baskets or tubs and begin organizing materials for the baskets. Other essential ingredients are a labeler, three rolls of labeling tape (yellow, red, and blue), four packages each of plain 4" x 6" index cards (one blue and one white), and library passes. This chapter will help you get your baskets ready for exploration, give you ideas for students to share their basket creations, and provide suggestions for evaluation.

## The Baskets

Any kind of plastic basket or tub (12" x 14") will suffice as long as it has room for 8½" x 11" worksheets, a few books, and other materials. These containers can be found at discount stores and grocery stores. Watch for the sales.

## Thinking Skills

Thinking is a mental process we all share, yet in different ways and to varying degrees. While some children concentrate on mastering basic knowledge, others are able to apply easily obtained information and channel this data in their own unique way. Gifted children generally demonstrate higher level thinking abilities and use their mental processes to create and imagine unusual thoughts. A curriculum for the gifted needs to ensure the use of both convergent and divergent thinking skills. Dr. Benjamin Bloom's Taxonomy of Educational Objectives (Bloom, 1956) is a model that provides definitions of six levels of thinking, questions, cues, and suggested media for the development of these processes.

The baskets can be labeled with colored tape according to the level of thinking skills listed in Bloom's Taxonomy. The six levels of thinking skills are knowledge, comprehension, application, analysis, synthesis, and evaluation. Most classroom instruction involves knowledge and comprehension. Therefore, basket activities should concentrate on the higher level thinking skills: application, analysis, synthesis, and evaluation.

Content in the baskets that focuses mainly on application should be labeled with the title of the basket on yellow tape; content that focuses on the thinking skills of analysis and synthesis should be labeled on red tape; and the highest level of thinking, evaluation, should be labeled on blue tape.

The purpose of color-coding the baskets according to thinking skills is so the teacher will know the level of skill that the student is working on. Your more capable students should eventually be concentrating on those baskets color-coded red and blue. If the teacher discovers that a highly capable student concentrates on the yellow-coded baskets, it is time for encouraging the student to move

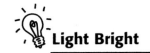
on to a red- or blue-coded basket. On the other hand, you may be pleasantly surprised to discover a student of lower capability working very successfully on a blue-coded basket. Color-coding is for teacher information only and does not need to be explained to students. From past experience, students usually are not interested in the color tape, but soon discover that red and blue coded baskets are "harder."

# Bloom's Taxonomy
## of Educational Objectives

**Knowledge:**
- Knows common terms.
- Knows specific facts.
- Knows methods/procedures.
- Knows basic concepts.

**Processes**–ask, match, discover, identify, listen, locate observe, define, describe, name, outline, list, read.
**Media**–record or compact disc, film, book, radio, television, model, magazine, encyclopedia, multiple choice, matching, and true-false exercise.
**Questions**–who, when, where, which, what.

**Comprehension:**
- Understands facts/principals.
- Interprets verbal material.
- Interprets charts/graphs.
- Translates verbal material into mathematical formulas.
- Estimates future consequences implied in data.
- Justifies methods/procedures.

**Processes**–explain, generalize, give examples, infer, paraphrase, predict, summarize, rewrite, describe, interpret, label, question, respond.
**Media**–essay, chart, graph, cartoon, speech, paragraph, verbal illustration.
**Questions**–compare and contrast, what is an analogy to, what does it mean, tell in your own words.

**Application:**
- Applies concepts/principles to new situations.
- Applies laws/theories to situations.
- Solves mathematical problems.
- Constructs charts/graphs.
- Demonstrates correct usage of a method/procedure.

**Processes**–demonstrate, apply, solve, use, teach, do, experiment, simulate, construct, operate, sequence, brainstorm, interpret.
**Media**–map, puzzle, model, problem, graph, chart, diagram.
**Questions**–how can you use it, where does it lead you, how does it apply.

**Analysis:**
- Recognizes unstated assumptions.
- Recognizes logical fallacies in reasoning.
- Distinguishes between facts/inferences.
- Evaluates the relevancy of data.
- Analyzes the organizational structure of a work (art, music, writing).

**Processes**–classify, categorize, separate, dissect, analyze, survey, diagram, compare, contrast, differentiate, relate.
**Media**–questionnaire, chart, diagram, music, literature, art, commercial, advertisement.
**Questions**–how, why, what are the causes, what are the steps of the process, how would you start, list all problems.

Classroom

Yellow

Red

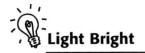 

**Synthesis:**

- Writes a well-organized theme.
- Gives a well-organized speech.
- Writes a creative short story (or poem or music).
- Proposes a plan for an experiment.

**Processes**–combine, invent, compose, role-play, produce, write, create, design, develop, hypothesize, conceptualize, refine.

**Media**–invention, product, game, piece of literature, piece of art, piece of music, plan, pantomime, article, commercial.

**Questions**–suppose, how many ways are possible, think of all the different, how else, what would happen if.

**Red**

**Evaluation:**

- Judges the logical consistency of written material.
- Judges the adequacy with which conclusions are supported by data.
- Judges the value of a work (art, music, writing) by use of internal criteria.
- Judges the value of a work (art, music, writing) by use of external standards of excellence.

**Processes**–evaluate, judge, debate, discuss, choose, rate, recommend, decide rank, predict, criticize.

**Media**–self-evaluation, decision, essay, debate, panel, group, discussion, trial.

**Questions**–set standards, which is good, what is the problem, will it work, decide which.

**Blue**

Basket materials are changed quarterly as new topics are introduced and the level of difficulty of materials advances. As students master basic skills, they are challenged by more sophisticated concepts. Parent-compiled baskets are added, as well as new art, writing, mathematics, and science activities. Children like making baskets and contributing their items and worksheets for other students to complete. Some baskets are very popular, and you may need to leave them at the center for two quarters. Seasonal activities are changed accordingly.

## Introducing Children to the Baskets

Introduce Light Bright baskets to your students at the beginning of the school year and at the beginning of each quarter as materials change. You are responsible for introducing your class to *Light Bright* (Classroom Model). As a grade level, set aside one week of afternoons during the second week of school as basket exploration time. Bring five to eight baskets into your classroom, introduce the materials, and read the directions for each basket. Divide the class into groups and set aside time to examine the contents of the baskets, ask questions, and participate in some of the activities. At the sound of a bell, each group moves to a different basket. Giving the children time to explore the basket materials not only arouses enthusiasm, but also provides for less confusion once the students are at the Light Bright Center.

While you are explaining the basket contents, five main Light Bright rules need to be stressed:

1. All basket materials are treated carefully and with respect. There is absolutely no throwing of materials, taking materials, or destroying materials in any way.
2. No more than two students are allowed to work on one basket at the same time.
3. No student has the right to tamper with any other student's work area or project.
4. Talking quietly is permitted.
5. Once you are done with a basket, all materials must be put back neatly and returned to the shelf.

Some role-playing of potential problems would be appropriate here—for example, messy baskets, other people intruding on another's work area, and missing materials. You may want to post these rules at the Light Bright Center.

During the same week that the materials are introduced, Student Expectations and Requirements for Light Bright participation (Chapter 2) need to be introduced and reviewed. Elaborate on the consequences of not following the rules.

Explain to the children that instructions for the baskets can be found on the white and blue note cards in each basket. Explain that students must complete the white note card before moving on to a blue note card, and that some baskets have more than one blue note card. At this time, teachers may have the entire class make a white note card activity, which usually is a project that takes no more than 20–30 minutes to complete. The next day, the entire class could make a blue note card activity, a project that may take several days or weeks to complete.

Explain that students can select the same basket more than once to work on, but they can make the white note card activity only once and must move on to the blue note card activities. The white note card activity is designed to introduce the concept and basket materials to the students. The blue note cards are designed to involve students in the higher level thinking skills.

Warning: If students complete only white note card activities, your Light Bright Center will become an arts and crafts center. Neat Idea: Put note cards on key chains to prevent loss or mix-ups.

Keep in mind that the materials provide tools for research and, eventually, sophisticated problem solving. However, if you or the volunteer see that a certain student is always picking the game basket or the art basket, it is time to suggest another activity on the space provided on the Light Bright Messages (Chapter 1).

After Light Bright has become familiar to the children, ask the volunteers to come in and introduce themselves. Have the volunteers emphasize that they know the Light Bright rules and, if they have any problem with misbehavior, it will be reported to the classroom teacher. Role-play children getting the light bulb, putting it on their desk, going to the Light Bright Center, and helping the volunteer fill out the Light Bright Messages.

Taking the time to explore the baskets; discussing the rules, expectations, requirements, and the consequences for not following the rules; role-playing; and meeting the volunteers will enable the center to run smoothly once it is open. The classroom teacher will not want to be bothered by petty problems occurring at the Light Bright Center.

## Criteria for Basket Contents

The materials you choose to put in the baskets depend on resources available to you. Suggested basket materials are included in Chapter 5.

Basket contents should not be busy, buy-time worksheets or any kind of repetitious work papers. The goal of Light Bright materials is to provide students with stimulating, thought-provoking activities that foster creativity, originality, and higher level thinking skills.

Criteria to use in evaluating whether the contents are appropriate for Light Bright baskets are included here. Materials should:

- provide hands-on activities;
- concentrate on higher levels of Bloom's Taxonomy;
- promote as much problem solving/thinking as possible;
- allow a student to exercise creativity and originality by having a visual product to share;
- have high interest for appropriate age level (see Chapter 4, "Student Interest Survey");
- come from a variety of content and talent areas;
- encourage the development of products that use new techniques, materials, and forms; and
- develop research skills and methods, independent or self-directed study skills.

## Sharing the Creation

During the week that you introduce the baskets to the children, tell them that a visual creation must result from a Light Bright experience with the exception of the computer and a few of the games. It may be a creation that takes only one session to complete, or, as the level of difficulty of materials increases, it may be a project that takes weeks to complete. All creations may either be shared verbally or displayed in some manner. Although sharing can take many forms, a visual product is evidence of a constructive learning experience. It is important to emphasize that the Light Bright Center is a fun place to be, but the constructive learning experience is essential.

Verbal sharing nurtures communication skills, provides opportunities for evaluation (feedback from other students), and encourages leadership characteristics to blossom. Creations can be shared with the student's own class, another class at the same grade level, or a different grade level. A special Light Bright open house is a great public relations event and offers the students an opportunity to share their creations with parents and the community.

## Kids Teaching Day

The idea of sharing verbally evolved into Kids Teaching Day at our school. We set aside time each Wednesday and Friday afternoon for students to share their Light Bright inventions and to give them an opportunity to be teachers. Wednesday's session focused on students sharing something they had created at Light Bright and asking fellow students for their opinions, suggestions for improvement, and generally discussing the concept behind the project. A warning: Most younger children will say, "I really like it." It is up to the teacher to encourage the child who responds with such an answer to state at least one reason why he or she likes it. The Wednesday sharing session provides a way for students to self-evaluate their creations. If, after discussing it with peers, a child feels that the project could be improved, then encourage that child to do so the next time he or she visits Light Bright. This process indicates self-growth and involves Bloom's highest thinking level of evaluation.

Friday's Kids Teaching Day evolved into students teaching a lesson of their choice. It all started when the children in my class became so intrigued with the drawings that Christina was bringing back from the Light Bright Center that they wanted to know how she drew them. I gave her half an hour to teach the children, and step-by-step she showed them how to draw the most fantastic cat. The children followed her every step on their papers. The only materials needed for her lesson were pencils and paper. In successive lessons, she taught them how to draw objects with shadows and depth perception. Christina was not only sharing her talent, but gaining self-confidence and enhancing her leadership characteristics, as well.

Kids Teaching Day turned out to be a hit. Within a week, 20 children had signed up for this special event. For your Kids Teaching Day, post a sign-up sheet next to the light bulbs and allow two children to sign up for each hour. On the sign-up sheet, provide space for the lesson topic, the date, and the materials needed. The way the children teach their lesson is totally up to them with little guidance from you. While the child is teaching the lesson, he or she may need your assistance with materials and perhaps some help in clarifying explanations.

We had all kinds of Kids Teaching Day topics. Richard, who is a gifted musician and plays the violin for the symphony, had the children diagram a violin and label the parts. He concluded with playing his violin for an awestruck audience. Emily taught the students how to write a story using a five-step process. Jennifer demonstrated how to grow a crystal garden and concluded her lesson with handing out the recipe to the class.

On another unforgettable day, Jason brought his live boa constrictor to school and taught a lesson on all-you-want-to-know-about-snakes-and-more! (We don't advise allowing children to bring their pets to school, however.) Children shared their hobbies such as coin or stamp collecting and described how others could have the same hobby. The list goes on. Once again, you will welcome these young children's expertise on such subjects as violins, drawing, snakes, and dinosaurs. Few of us can claim we have as much knowledge as they do.

## Ideas for Final Products

As you begin to put together materials for your baskets, keep possibilities in mind for end products and creative methods for communicating the concept gained from the basket materials. The ideas presented here work well for Light Bright Centers. You can encourage the children to come up with their own ideas—often theirs are better than ours.

# Bright Ideas for Original Projects

- ❏ Advertisement
- ❏ Autobiography
- ❏ Booklet
- ❏ Cartoon
- ❏ Chart
- ❏ Collages
- ❏ Collection
- ❏ Dance
- ❏ Debate
- ❏ Demonstration
- ❏ Diorama
- ❏ Drawing
- ❏ Fact File
- ❏ Flip Book
- ❏ Flannel Board Story
- ❏ Food Preparation
- ❏ Game
- ❏ Graph
- ❏ Graphic
- ❏ Greeting Card
- ❏ Invention
- ❏ Interview
- ❏ Jig Saw Puzzle
- ❏ Journal
- ❏ Labeled Diagram
- ❏ Lithograph
- ❏ Magazine
- ❏ Map
- ❏ Mobile

- ❏ Model
- ❏ Movie in a Box
- ❏ Multimedia Presentation
- ❏ Mural
- ❏ Musical Instrument
- ❏ Newspaper Article
- ❏ Painting
- ❏ Photo Essay
- ❏ Play
- ❏ Poem
- ❏ Poster
- ❏ Puppet Show
- ❏ Report
- ❏ Riddle
- ❏ Sand Casting
- ❏ Scrap Book
- ❏ Sculpture
- ❏ Skit
- ❏ Song
- ❏ Speech
- ❏ Survey
- ❏ Tape Recording
- ❏ Teach a Lesson
- ❏ Terrarium
- ❏ Timeline
- ❏ Transparency
- ❏ Travel Log
- ❏ Video
- ❏ Web Page

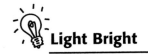 

## Evaluation

Light Bright creations should not be graded. The evaluation on the Light Bright Messages (Chapter 1, Figure 2) is adequate. Students are evaluated by the school, parents, teachers, and peers so constantly that many children become afraid to act on their own accord, let alone be truly creative. Light Bright should give children an opportunity to express themselves freely without having to worry about criticism. After all, the student will be his or her most severe critic.

You want to create an emotionally supportive environment at the Light Bright Center. Encourage students to move toward creative risk taking and experimentation and away from old blocks and fears. If children know ahead of time that there will not be a grade on their creations, they will feel free to create in their own unique way. Although there will be guidelines to follow, each student will experience a basket in a little different way and, thus, should have a unique creation.

Assessment and planning forms are included here for rating a Light Bright product, as well as a student evaluation form for students to rate their own creations and a writing checklist. Notice that the assessment form is rated, not graded.

**Warning**: Please be very sensitive to the young, creative soul.

# Light Bright
# Student Assessment and
# Planning Forms

# My Project Plan

Date: _____

Creator: _____

What I plan to do: _____

_____

_____

How I will share my project: _____

_____

_____

Signature: _____

- - - - - - - - - - - - - - - - - - - - - - - - - - - - - - - - - - - - - - - - - - - - - - - - - - - - - - -

# My Project Plan

Date: _____

Creator: _____

What I plan to do: _____

_____

_____

How I will share my project: _____

_____

_____

Signature: _____

# **Plan for My Light Bright Project**

**Name:** _____

**Teacher:** _____

**Date:** _____  **Project title:** _____

Goal (What I plan to make): _____

_____

_____

_____

_____

Materials (What I plan to use): _____

_____

_____

_____

_____

Plan (Steps I will take to make the project): _____

_____

_____

_____

_____

Expected date of completion: _____

**Light Bright
Creation Assessment Form**

Name(s): _____

Teacher: _____

Date: _____ Number of Days Worked on Project _____

Creation (Title and/or brief description): _____

_____

| Overall Assessment of Creation | Rating | Not Applicable |
|---|---|---|
| 1. Innovative ideas | _____ | _____ |
| 2. Depth and complexity of completion | _____ | _____ |
| 3. Overall appearance of creation | _____ | _____ |
| 4. Organization of creation | _____ | _____ |
| 5. Amount of effort involved | _____ | _____ |
| 6. Many resources used | _____ | _____ |

**Overall Assessment of Work Habits**

| | | |
|---|---|---|
| 7. Works independently | _____ | _____ |
| 8. Displays task commitment | _____ | _____ |
| 9. Works at accelerated rate | _____ | _____ |
| 10. Works cooperatively | _____ | _____ |

**TOTAL POINTS** _____

**Rating Scale Comments:**
1—Needs Improvement   3—Good
2—Fair                4—Superior

**Person completing this form:** _____

# Light Bright
# Student Evaluation Form

**Name:** _____

**Teacher:** _____

**Date:** _____

**Title of creation:** _____  **Basket title:** _____

Do I feel that my Light Bright creation is:    ❑ Unique    ❑ Ordinary

Did I use my time wisely?    ❑ Yes    ❑ No

Do I like my Light Bright creation?    ❑ Yes    ❑ No

If yes, why? _____

If no, why not?_____

Did I learn something new?    ❑ Yes    ❑ No

If yes, what new information did I learn?_____

_____

If no, what do I want to learn more about? _____

_____

Did I enjoy my project?    ❑ Yes    ❑ No

Why or why not? _____

Is my work neat?    ❑ Yes    ❑ No

How do I plan to share my Light Bright project with others? _____

_____

_____

**Light Bright Writing Checklist**

**Author:** _____

**Teacher:** _____

**Date:** _____

**Title of story:** _____

Check (✔) the correct answer.

Did I:

|   |   |   |   |   |
|---|---|---|---|---|
| 1. | capitalize my sentences and use periods? | ❑ Yes | ❑ No |
| 2. | have a beginning, middle, and ending to my story? | ❑ Yes | ❑ No |
| 3. | use a lot of "ands" and "buts" that I didn't need to use? | ❑ Yes | ❑ No |
| 4. | have one main idea in a paragraph? | ❑ Yes | ❑ No |
| 5. | have at least three sentences in a paragraph? | ❑ Yes | ❑ No |
| 6. | indent my paragraphs? | ❑ Yes | ❑ No |
| 7. | look up words that I didn't know how to spell? | ❑ Yes | ❑ No |
| 8. | have a title for my story? | ❑ Yes | ❑ No |
| 9. | have pictures for my story? | ❑ Yes | ❑ No |
| 10. | proofread and rewrite? | ❑ Yes | ❑ No |
| 11. | like what I wrote? | ❑ Yes | ❑ No |
| 12. | Do you want to write again? | ❑ Yes | ❑ No |

If yes, write five things you might want to write about:

1. _____

2. _____

3. _____

4. _____

5. _____

# Light Bright Center Checklist: Steps to Take Now

**Phase I—Basket Exploration Activities**       **Done**

1. Select a place or format for the center. ❏

2. Build shelving, post rules, and decorate the center. ❏

3. Purchase 20–25 baskets/tubs, labeler, three rolls of labeling tape (yellow, red, blue), packages of 4" x 6" plain white and blue index cards, key rings. ❏

4. Purchase or copy materials for baskets. (Materials in Chapter 5 of the manual will get you started.) ❏

5. Assemble and label baskets, photocopy, cut, and glue note card directions and extensions onto the note cards, laminate, and attach to key rings. (Good job for volunteers!) ❏

6. Photocopy worksheets for baskets. (Copies in manual.) ❏

7. Make yellow light bulbs, photocopy Information Messages (copies in manual). Hang the light bulbs in the classroom and place a basket nearby for completed student Information Messages. ❏

8. Send out Parent/Community Interest Letter and Survey. (Copies in manual.) ❏

9. When surveys are returned, compile a master list for Phases I, II, and III. ❏

10. Schedule a Volunteer Meeting. (See manual for instructions.) ❏

11. Select a Light Bright Volunteer Coordinator who is in charge of scheduling volunteers for each phase. ❏

12. Post volunteer time schedule at the center. ❏

13. Demonstrate Light Bright Baskets in the classroom. ❏

14. Administer Student Interest Survey. (Copy in manual.) ❏

# Chapter 4:
# Gathering Materials

Chapter 4 will discuss the variety of resources available to teachers interested in gifted or enrichment material. The resources listed are not comprehensive, but are ones that will help you in establishing a Light Bright Center. Many materials are created from teacher, parent, or student imagination. Once you have established your basket center, you will begin to look at the world in a different way. As you walk into the dollar store, visit an arts and crafts fair, attend a play, or take classes, you will begin to view these experiences as ideas for baskets. Some call it "Basket Fever!"

Talented students should be encouraged to submit their most outstanding pieces for possible publication. This chapter contains a list of publishers who specialize in printing children's original works.

## On Your Own

Have you ever had a gifted program at your school? If so, find those materials and use them at the Light Bright Center. Do you have resource coordinators in your school district? They can be very helpful in providing materials. Your librarian undoubtedly has a wealth of materials. Remember those items collecting dust on the top shelf in the library? Brush off the dust and use them at Light Bright. *National Geographic* kits, book club materials, art and music books, and science kits are but a few resources for finding Light Bright materials. Children's book clubs, such as Troll Books, provide excellent materials for starting baskets.

Go to the teachers of the next grade level and pool their resources, too. Go through your Parent/Community Interest Surveys and ask a parent or a community member to bring in hobby or interest materials to duplicate for a Light Bright basket. Students interested in the same topic may want to put a basket together as a Light Bright project.

You can also put problem-solving games like Battleship®, checkers, or chess in a basket. These games may inspire students to create their own games. With a bit of creativity and research, you will find that you have enough materials in your own school to open a Light Bright Center without much investment for materials.

Many texts and teachers' manuals contain material explicitly designed to foster thinking skills. Unfortunately, it often comes at the end of the chapter. As teachers desperately try to get through the textbook in what never seems to be enough time, they may skip this very important part of learning. Light Bright offers a wonderful opportunity to integrate these materials into baskets.

## Beautiful Junk Box

How can any teacher manage a classroom without a beautifully decorated junk box filled with odds and ends? Many elementary teachers send an introductory letter home prior to the beginning of school that includes school supplies needed for the year. This is a great time to let students and parents know that you have a Beautiful Junk Box in your classroom and request that parents never again throw away another toilet paper roll, plastic bottle, coffee can, or other bits and pieces that students can use in constructing their Light Bright projects. State that you will need this "junk" for a very special program that will start later in the year (the Light Bright Program, of course). Request that all items be clean and safe.

Suggested list of special things to save:

❑ berry baskets
❑ bottle caps
❑ boxes (small)
❑ buttons/beads/broken jewelry
❑ cardboard tubes
❑ clothes pins
❑ coffee cans
❑ corks
❑ cottage cheese containers
❑ cotton balls
❑ feathers
❑ felt
❑ frozen juice cans
❑ magnets
❑ margarine tubs
❑ nuts and bolts
❑ old puzzle pieces
❑ old shirts for smocks
❑ old toy pieces

❑ pie tins
❑ pine cones
❑ plastic lids
❑ popsicle sticks
❑ seeds
❑ shells
❑ shoe boxes
❑ socks
❑ spice jars and cans
❑ spools
❑ squeeze bottles
❑ string and yarn
❑ Styrofoam® meat trays
❑ Styrofoam® packing
❑ wallpaper samples
❑ wrapping paper
❑ wood blocks
❑ wood scraps
❑ yogurt containers

## Student Interest Surveys

Student Interest Surveys are filled out by students at the beginning of the school year. To complete Student Interest Surveys, read the questions aloud to your entire class as students fill in their answers. You may need some parent helpers to assist younger children write their responses.

After the Student Interest Forms are collected, the individual teacher notes the top three interest areas in that class. Teachers in each grade level then meet to compare classroom results and choose high-interest topics suitable for Light Bright. Then, it is a matter of pooling your resources to come up with materials to add to or complement the ones enclosed in this manual.

# Light Bright
# Student Interest Survey

**Name:** _____

1. Name two things you like to do best in your spare time:

   • _____

   • _____

2. Are you a collector? Do you collect coins, stamps, receipts, shells, insects, rocks, baseball cards, or other things? List the things you collect.

   • _____

   • _____

   • _____

   • _____

3. What do you want to be when you grow up?

   First Choice:_____

   Second Choice: _____

4. Pretend you could invite anyone in the world to be your teacher for one week. Who would you invite?

   First Choice:_____

   Second Choice: _____

5. What are two favorite games you like to play?

   • _____

   • _____

6. If you could invent anything in the world, what would you invent?

   • _____

   • _____

7.   If you could go anywhere in the world or the universe, where would you go?

_____

_____

8.   What are your favorite books?

_____

_____

9.   What are your favorite TV shows?

_____

_____

10.   Do you like to: (check all that apply)

| | | |
|---|---|---|
| Be in a play | ❑ Yes | ❑ No |
| Build models | ❑ Yes | ❑ No |
| Cook | ❑ Yes | ❑ No |
| Design costumes | ❑ Yes | ❑ No |
| Draw | ❑ Yes | ❑ No |
| Enter animal fairs | ❑ Yes | ❑ No |
| Enter contests | ❑ Yes | ❑ No |
| Learn a craft | ❑ Yes | ❑ No |
| Listen to music | ❑ Yes | ❑ No |
| Make up stories | ❑ Yes | ❑ No |
| Paint | ❑ Yes | ❑ No |
| Play an instrument | ❑ Yes | ❑ No |
| Pretend to be someone else | ❑ Yes | ❑ No |
| Repair broken things | ❑ Yes | ❑ No |
| Write poems | ❑ Yes | ❑ No |
| Write stories | ❑ Yes | ❑ No |

If you have a budget for gifted or enrichment materials, the following list of catalogs will provide you with a wealth of materials. Many of the catalogs focus on manipulative, creative problem-solving materials—perfect for Light Bright baskets.

## Catalogs

**Bantam Dell Publishing Group, Inc.**
P.O. Box 7777W0175
Philadelphia, PA 19175-0175
Phone: (888) 232-7733
Fax: (703) 264-9494
www.randomhouse.com

**Council for Exceptional Children (CEC)**
1110 N. Glebe Rd., Suite 300
Arlington, VA 22201-5704
Phone: (888) 232-7733
Fax: (703) 264-9494
www.cec.sped.org

**Creative Publications**
5623 W. 115th St.
Alsip, IL 60803
Phone: (800) 624-0822
Fax: (800) 624-0821
www.creativepublications.com

**Critical Thinking Books & Software**
P.O. Box 448
Pacific Grove, CA 93950-0448
Phone: (800) 458-4849
Fax: (831) 393-3277
www.criticalthinking.com

**Dandy Lion Publications**
3563 Sueldo, Suite L
San Luis Obispo, CA 93401
Phone: (800) 776-8032
Fax: (805) 544-2823
www.dandylionbooks.com

**Dover Publications**
31 E 2nd St.
Mineola, NY 11501
Phone: (516) 294-7000
www.doverpublications.com

**Educational Impressions**
210 Sixth Ave.
Hawthorne, NJ 07507
Phone: (800) 451-7450
Fax: (201) 423-5569
www.ed-pak.com

**Free Spirit Publishing**
217 Fifth Ave. N, Suite 200
Minneapolis, MN 55401-1299
Phone: (800) 735-7323
Fax: (612) 337-5050
www.freespirit.com

**Fun Publishing Company**
2121 Alpine Place, #402
Cincinnati, OH 45206-2602
Phone: (513) 533-3636
Fax: (513) 421-7269
www.funpublishing.com

**The Great Books Foundation**
35 E Wacker Dr., Suite 2300
Chicago, IL 60601-2298
Phone: (800) 222-5870
Fax: (312) 407-0334
www.greatbooks.org

**Greenleaf Press**
3761 Hwy 109 N
Lebanon, TN 37087
Phone: (615) 449-1617
www.greenleafpress.com

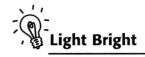 

**Highlights Catalog**
2300 Hidden Picture Dr.
P.O. Box 1450
Columbus, OH 43216-1450
www.highlightsforchildren.com

**MindWare**
121 5th Ave. NW
New Brighton, MN 55112
Phone: (800) 299-9273
Fax: (888) 274-9273
www.mindwareonline.com

**National Association for Gifted Children**
1707 L St. NW, Suite 550
Washington, DC 20036
Phone: (202) 785-4268
Fax: (202) 785-4248
www.nagc.org

**New Horizons for Learning**
P.O. Box 15329
Seattle, WA 98115
Phone: (206) 547-7936
Fax: (206) 726-0218
www.newhorizons.org

**Pieces of Learning**
1990 Market Rd.
Marion, IL 62959
Phone: (800) 729-5137
Fax: (800) 844-0455
www.piecesoflearning.com

**Prufrock Press, Inc.**
P.O. Box 8813
Waco, TX 76714-8813
Phone: (800) 998-2208
Fax: (800) 240-0333
www.prufrock.com

**Penguin USA**
375 Hudson St.
New York, NY 10014-3657
Phone: (212) 366-2493

Fax: (212) 366-2060
www.penguin.com/usa

**Scholastic Inc.**
555 Broadway
New York, NY 10012-3999
Phone: (800) SCHOLASTIC
www.scholastic.com

**Simon & Schuster**
**Children's Publishing Division**
200 Old Tappan Rd.
Old Tappan, NJ 07675-7095
Phone: (800) 223-2348
Fax: (800) 223-2336
www.simonandschuster.com

**Troll Book Club**
100 Corporate Dr.
Mahwah, NJ 07430-9986
Phone: (888) 99-TROLL
Fax: (888) 71-TROLL
www.troll.com

**Zephyr Press**
3316 N Chapel Ave.
Tucson, AZ 85716-1416
Phone: (800) 232-2187
Fax: (520) 232-9402
www.zephyrpress.com

## Magazines—Some publish student work

**Boys Life/S306**
P.O. Box 152079
Irving, TX 75015-2079
www.scouting.org/mags/boyslife
Age: Boys 6–18

**Challenge**
**c/o Frank Schaffer Publications**
23740 Hawthorne Blvd.
Torrance, CA 90505-5927
Phone: (800) 421-5533
www.frankschaffer.com
Age: Pre-K–Grade 8

**Children's Playmate**
P.O. Box 420234
Palm Coast, FL 32142-0234
www.cbhi.org
Age: 6–8

**Creative Kids**
P.O. Box 8813
Waco, TX 76714-8813
Phone: (800) 998-2208
Fax: (800) 240-0333
www.prufrock.com
Age: 8–14

**Cricket Magazine**
P.O. Box 300
Peru, IL 61354
www.cricketmag.com
Ages: 9–14

**Dolphin Log**
**The Cousteau Society**
870 Greenbrier Cir., Suite 402
Chesapeake, VA 23320
Phone: (800) 441-4395
www.dolphinlog.com
Age: 5–12

**Girl's Life Magazine**
4517 Harford Rd.
Baltimore, MD 21214
Phone: (888) 999-3222
www.girlslife.com
Age: 10–14

**Highlights for Children**
803 Church St.

Honesdale, PA 18431
Phone: (800) 603-0349
www.highlightsforchildren.com
Age: 2–12

**Humpty Dumpty's Magazine**
P.O. Box 420234
Palm Coast, FL 32142-0234
www.cbhi.org
Age: 4–6

**Jack and Jill**
P.O. Box 420234
Palm Coast, FL 32142-0234
www.cbhi.org
Age: 6–8

**National Geographic Magazine**
P.O. Box 98199
Washington, DC 20090-6095
Phone: (800) 447-0647
www.nationalgeographic.com

**New Moon**
P.O. Box 3620
Duluth, MN 55803
Phone: (800) 381-4743
Fax: (218) 728-0314
www.newmoon.org
Age: Girls 8–14

**Owl**
179 John St, Suite 500
Toronto, ON M5T, 3G5
Phone: (800) 551-6957
www.owl.on.ca
Age: 8 & Up

**Ranger Rick**
P.O. Box 2049
Harlan, IA 51593-0269
Phone: (800) 611-1599
www.nwf.org/kids
Age: 7–12

**Spider**
P.O. Box 300
Peru, IL 61354
www.cricketmag.com
Ages: 6–9

**Stone Soup Magazine**
P.O. Box 83
Santa Cruz, CA 95063
Phone: (800) 447-4569
Fax: (831) 426-1161
www.stonesoup.com
Age: Through Age 13

**Young Author's Magazines**
Reulus Communications, Inc.
3015 Woodsdale Blvd.
Lincoln, NE 68502-5053
Phone: (402) 450-1252
Fax: (402) 421-9682
www.yam.regulus.com
Age: K–12

**U.S. Kids**
P.O. Box 420234
Palm Coast, FL 32142-0234
www.cbhi.org
Age: 6–11

## Supplies

**Highsmith, Inc.**
W5527 Hwy 106
P.O. Box 800
Fort Atkinson, WI 53538-080
Phone: (800) 554-4661
Fax: (800) 558-9332
Hang Up Media Bags

# Chapter 5:
# Basket Activities

Suggested basket activities fall into the following categories: art, drama, language arts and reading, mathematics, research, inventions, games, and science. Neither the activities nor the categories presented here are inclusive. For example, music and the natural and social sciences would be other wonderful areas to explore. The ideas suggested here have been tried at Light Bright Centers and have proven to be appropriate. Your baskets may be different depending upon your resources, student interests, and talents.

Each basket plan includes required materials, teacher preparation (which can be done by volunteers), and directions for students. The directions for students are either on the basket worksheet or on 4" x 6" white or blue note cards. If the directions are to be put on note cards, copy the page, cut out, and glue the directions onto the note card, then laminate. The directions for the initial project go on white note cards; directions for extensions of the same activity go on blue note cards. Extension activities are more complex, but keep to the theme of the basket. For younger students, you may enlarge the note cards at least 50% on a copier.

The thinking levels according to Bloom's Taxonomy and the skills used to complete the lesson plan are indicated at the end of each activity. When assessing whether or not the student has mastered the objective/concept of the activity, keep in mind that the goal is to allow students to apply and build on higher level thinking skills and to foster creativity and originality.

Some of the lesson plans include worksheets and/or figures. Teachers find it helpful to photocopy all of the worksheets and figures as master copies. The masters are kept in a file at the Light Bright Center for easy access.

# Art

Cartoons • Drawings • God's Eye Weaving • Noodle Designs • Origami

Basket activities for arts and crafts are included in this section. A true artist may dispute whether crafts should be included with art. A craft experience tends to lend itself to a step-by-step sequence that results in a product. However, when the students learn the basic procedure of creating the craft, they can then use the process of creativity to design and build an original craft. An art experience does not necessarily have to result in a product that pleases anyone but the artist. The activities in this section are designed to give your students creative experiences that are blended with skill-building procedures.

> A newspaper editor fired
> Walt Disney because he had
> "no good ideas."

**Basket Materials:**
- Cartoon Worksheet
- Comic strips from newspapers
- Pencils
- Erasers
- Crayons or felt-tipped markers

**Preparation:** Label basket *Cartoons* with red tape. Photocopy about 10 cartoon worksheets. Put worksheets in basket along with other materials. Your class may want to start a collection of old photographs at the beginning of the school year (see Extension).

**Directions:** Copy the following on a white 4" x 6" note card, then laminate.

**Directions:**                                  **Cartoons**
1. Take some time to read the comic strips. You will notice that some comic strips begin with a funny problem and end with a funny or odd solution that makes you laugh. Other cartoons show a funny situation. Riddles and jokes make good cartoons, too.
2. Draw some characters for your cartoon and think of something funny they can say or do.
3. Color your cartoon.
4. Have a good laugh and share your cartoon with your class so they can laugh, too.

**Extension:** Copy the following on a blue 4" x 6" note card, then laminate.

**Extension:**                                  **Cartoons**
1. Ask your parents for some old photographs they don't need or want anymore.
2. Use faces or parts of the photographs to make a comic strip.
3. Be sure that your characters say something and that your comic strip has a beginning and an ending.

**Thinking Levels:** Application, Analysis, Synthesis

**Skills:**
- Creates a form of art
- Applies and demonstrates methods and principles of cartooning/drawing
- Invents own comic strip

**Basket Materials:**
- Drawing booklet
- Large-sized graph paper (1" x 1" squares)
- Drawing paper
- Pencils
- Erasers
- Crayons or felt-tipped markers

**Preparation:** Label basket *Drawing* with red tape. Bind the booklet with three binder rings and laminate. Place the booklet in the basket together with other materials.

**Directions:** Copy the following on a white 4" x 6" note card, then laminate.

**Directions:**                                              **Drawing**
Instructions are included in the booklet.

**Extension:** Copy the following on a blue 4" x 6" note card, then laminate.

**Extension:**                                              **Drawing**
1. Draw your own picture freehand. (Do not use graph paper.)
2. Color your picture with crayons, markers, chalk, or paint.
3. Have the helper mount it on black construction paper and laminate it for you.
4. Display it on bulletin board.

**Thinking Levels:** Application, Analysis

**Skills:**
- Applies concepts and basic principles of drawing
- Creates original drawing
- Analyzes spatial relationships

# Draw and Enjoy

Drawing is a most satisfactory hobby. Anyone of any age can draw pictures any time and anywhere. You don't need to have fancy equipment—paper and pencil work fine. Make it a habit to always carry and use a small sketching notebook. Drawing regularly helps you become a better observer and makes you more aware of the world around you.

**Do your own thing in drawing.**

There is no need to try to copy pictures exactly. Learn to draw what *you* see as you see it. This is creativity.

In this drawing booklet, you will begin by practicing basic forms. Always look for the basic form (or forms) in the objects you plan to draw.

After you have practiced drawing basic forms and some of the shape objects, you are ready to practice drawing on graph paper. Look at the Human Head and Horses drawings on the next two pages in the drawing booklet. Observe how the parts of each picture rest on the graph paper squares. Try to copy these pictures exactly. This practice will help you with spacing in your drawings.

The rest of the booklet will help give you some ideas of objects to draw. You may want to draw them on graph or drawing paper.

As you finish each of your drawings, you may color them, and the helper will file them for you. When you are all done with the booklet, the helper will bind your papers into your very own drawing booklet. You can then design and label your cover.

Now, you are ready to go on to the blue note card in the basket and really show off your artistic talent!

# Basic Forms

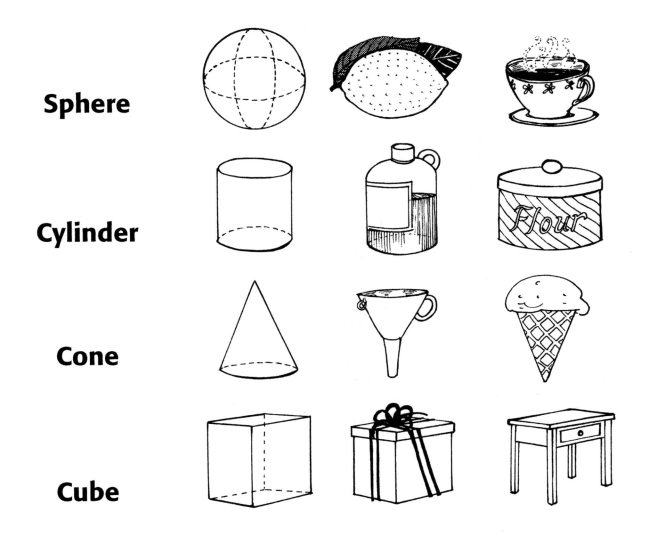

**Sphere**

**Cylinder**

**Cone**

**Cube**

On this page, you see four basic shapes and how these shapes appear in objects.

Practice drawing these shapes on graph paper. Then, draw the objects shown on this page or create some of your own using the basic shapes.

# The Human Head

As faces vary considerably, these measurement tips are only guidelines.

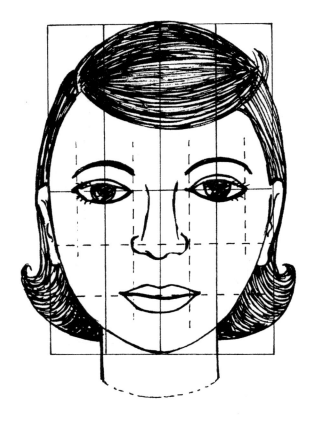

☞ The human head is an egg-shaped sphere on top of a short cylinder.

☞ The eyes are midway between the top of the head and the tip of the chin.

☞ The nose is 1/3 the distance from the eyes to the chin.

☞ The eyes are centered 1/4 of the distance between the middle of the nose and the outer edges of the face.

☞ The nostrils are as wide as the space between the eyes.

☞ The mouth is a little bit wider.

Most people's faces are different from one side to the other and are rarely symmetrical.

# Horses

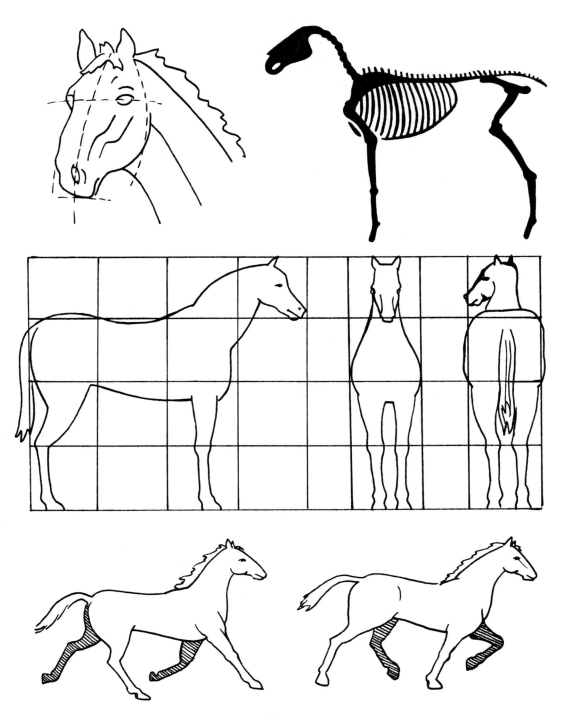

Horses' right legs move in opposition to their left legs.

# Fashion Dolls

Fashion dolls are at least nine heads high. They are very slender and stylized with very long legs and tiny hands and feet.

# Stuffed Animals

They are always cute, cuddly, often funny, and always fun to collect.

Such toys are usually made of "fake" fur, felt, or fabric.

They are great to draw as they are designed with considerable simplicity and use basic forms that are easy to identify.

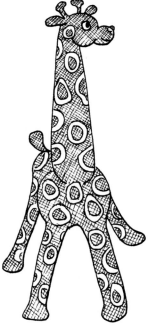

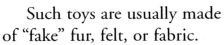

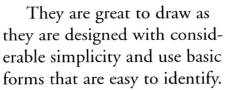

**Color Code: Red**

**Basket Materials:**
- God's Eye Weaving Worksheet
- Figures 6 & 7
- Balls of yarn in different colors
- Popsicle sticks
- Chop sticks or dowels
- Glue

**Preparation:** Label basket *God's Eye Weaving* with red tape. Place materials in basket. Glue Figures on white note cards, laminate, and place in basket. Make 10 copies of the God's Eye Weaving Worksheet onto blue paper and place in basket.

**Directions:** Copy the following on a white 4" x 6" note card, then laminate.

**Directions:**                                    **God's Eye Weaving**
1. Select two sticks and glue them together in the center to form a cross, with all four "arms" equal.
2. Take one end of the yarn and tie it around the center of the crossed sticks. Make a tight knot.
3. A basic weave is called the front wrap. Hold the sticks in one hand, keeping the sticks crossed, and hold the yarn in the other hand.
4. Weave the yarn over one arm, then under, around, and over the same arm (see Figure 6).
5. Go to the next arm and weave around it the same way—over the arm, under, around, and over. Always push the weave to the center.
6. When your weaving reaches almost to the end of the sticks, you are done. Finish the weaving by tying the end of the yarn around one of the arms (see Figure 7.)

**Extensions:** Copy the following on blue 4" x 6" note cards, then laminate.

**Extension I:**                                    **God's Eye Weaving**
1. Go to the library and look up the history of the God's Eye.
2. Write it down and report to your class the information you found.

**Extension II:**                                    **God's Eye Weaving**
1. Design and make an original tassel or object that you will attach to your God's Eye Weaving.
2. This attachment should have special meaning to you and your family.
3. Attach your invention to your weaving and hang it in a special place in your house.

**Thinking Levels:**     Analysis, Synthesis

**Skills:**
- Creates Pueblo and Mexican Indian art form
- Demonstrates correct methods of weaving
- Analyzes structure of an art form
- Writes a well-organized report

# History of the God's Eye Weaving

"Ojo de Dios" is the Spanish translation of the Huichol Indian word, "sikuli" or "eye of God." God's Eye Weavings are a form of Huichol Indian folk-art. To them, it is a symbol to protect and bless the home and to keep evil away.

A tuft of cotton-like substance from the squash blossom was sometimes attached to the end of the weaving to bring extra meaning to the blessing. In modern times, this has resulted in the attachment of a tassel to the weaving.

**Glue each figure on a 4" x 6" white note card, then laminate.**

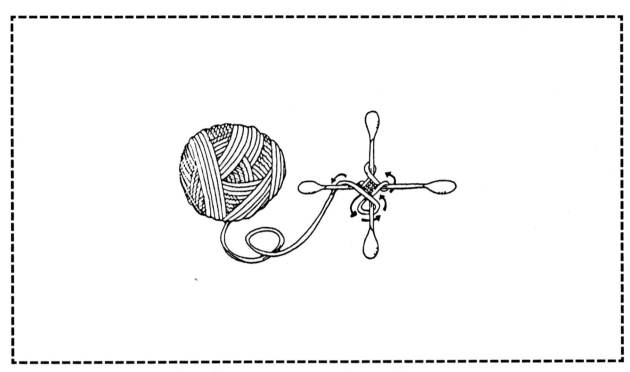

**Figure 6: Getting Started on a God's Eye Weave**

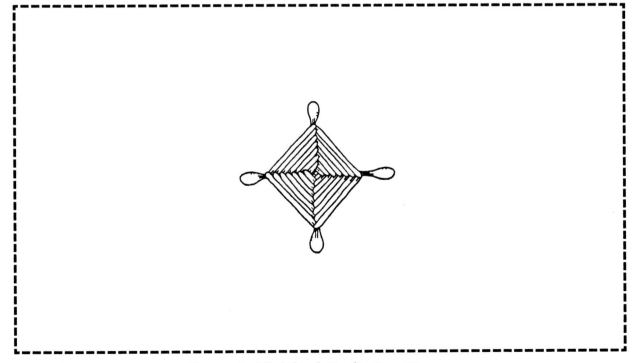

**Figure 7: Finished God's Eye Weave**

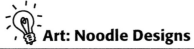 

**Color Code: Red**

| | |
|---|---|
| **Basket Materials:** | • Plastic baggies containing various kinds of noodles—macaroni, spaghetti, lasagna, bows, wheels, or any other kind of pasta<br>• Various kinds of dried beans can also be added<br>• Drawing paper<br>• Pencils<br>• Erasers<br>• Glue<br>• Various sizes of cardboard or poster board |
| **Preparation:** | Label basket *Noodle Designs* with red tape. Place pasta and beans in baggies and place in basket along with other materials. |
| **Directions:** | Copy the following on a white 4" x 6" note card, then laminate. |

**Directions:**                                          **Noodle Design**
1. Draw your own design on paper.
2. Lay out your design on cardboard using noodles and/or beans.
3. When you are satisfied with your design, glue it in place.

**Extension:**          Copy the following on a blue 4" x 6" note card, then laminate.

**Extension:**                                          **Noodle Design**
1. Try designing a new machine or a new kind of transportation on drawing paper.
2. Lay out your machine or form of transportation on cardboard using the noodles and/or beans. Glue it in place.
3. Describe your invention and how it works to your class. Ask them if they think it could really work. Why or why not? Then, state your opinion and explain.

**Thinking Levels:**          Analysis, Synthesis

**Skills:**
• Creates original design
• Designs own invention
• Evaluates feasibility of invention

| | |
|---|---|
| **Basket Materials:** | • Any educational Origami instruction booklet found in a stationery or book store<br>• Origami folding paper (or colored copy paper) cut into different sized squares<br>• Scissors |

**Preparation:**   Label basket *Origami* with red tape. Place materials in the basket.

**Directions:**   Copy the following on a white 4" x 6" note card, then laminate.

**Directions:**                                                                                   **Origami**
Instructions are included in the Origami instruction booklet.

**Extension:**   Copy the following on blue 4" x 6" note cards, then laminate.

**Extension I:**                                                                              **Origami**
1. Teach your class how to fold one of the Origami patterns that you like.
2. Sign up for Kids Teaching Day.
3. Have your teacher help you cut the paper for the project.
4. Can you invent an original Origami pattern? Try one. Teach the class your new pattern.

**Extension II:**                                                                             **Origami**
1. Design original Origami jewelry using Origami patterns. Some ideas: earrings, necklaces, bracelets, or pins.
2. Buy jewelry parts like loops for earrings at a craft store.
3. Decide on prices and sell your jewelry to friends or give as gifts.

**Thinking Levels:**   Analysis, Synthesis

**Skills:**
• Creates Japanese art form
• Demonstrates correct methods of paper folding
• Analyzes and teaches structure of a form of art
• Creates original product
• Demonstrates leadership

# Drama

Puppets • Puppet Play • TV Producer

Drama can easily be called *creative play*. Children in the elementary grades have vivid imaginations and have practiced creative play all of their lives, and so making up a skit, a play, or a puppet show is easy and natural for this age group. Give them a few puppets or props, and it does not take long for them to come up with a creation.

**Winston Churchill failed
the sixth grade.**

**Basket Materials:**
- Paper plates
- Felt-tipped pens
- Markers or crayons
- Tape
- Writing paper
- Pencils
- Scissors
- Popsicle sticks
- Scraps of cloth
- Yarn
- Construction paper scraps
- Ribbon
- Buttons
- Corks
- Sequins
- Stick-on stars
- Pipe cleaners
- Glue
- Anything else that could be used to decorate a puppet

**Preparation:** Label basket *Puppet* with red tape.

**Directions:** Copy the following on a white 4" x 6" note card, then laminate.

**Directions:**                                              **Puppets**
1. Take a paper plate and draw a face.
2. Decorate it with odds and ends from the basket. Use yarn for hair, mustaches, beards, shaggy eyebrows, and animal manes.
3. Curl thin strips of construction paper around pencils for curly hair. Pipe cleaners can be used for whiskers, corks for noses, cotton for fur, buttons or sequins for eyes. Use your imagination.
4. Tape the stick to the back of the paper plate.
5. Now, you have a puppet.
6. Write a paragraph about who your puppet is.
7. Share your puppet and your paragraph with your class.

**Extension:** Copy the following on a blue 4" x 6" note card, then laminate.

**Extension:**                                              **Puppets**
1. Meet with other students who have made paper plate puppets.
2. Create a puppet show together.
3. Plan and make a puppet stage.
4. Present your puppet play to a kindergarten class.

**Thinking Levels:** Analysis, Synthesis

**Color Code: Red**

**Skills:**

- Demonstrates understanding of puppet construction
- Creates original puppets
- Creates original puppet play
- Designs original puppet stage
- Exercises writing skills

**Basket Materials:**
- TV Producer Worksheets
- Scissors
- Crayons or felt-tipped markers
- Glue
- Filmstrip
- Colored pencils
- Tape recorder & blank tapes

**Preparation:**

Label basket *TV Producer* with red tape. Photocopy 10 copies of each worksheet and staple together in pairs. Place materials in basket.

**Directions:**

Copy the following on a white 4" x 6" note card, then laminate.

**Directions:**                                    **TV Producer**
Instructions are on worksheet.

**Extension:**

Copy the following on blue 4" x 6" note cards, then laminate.

**Extension I:**                                   **TV Producer**
1. Produce a real TV show. You may do this project at the Light Bright Center.
2. Decide what your show will be about.
3. Choose up to three actors for your show. (You may meet with these people at the Light Bright Center.)
4. Decide on a setting, costumes, and props.
5. Practice the show.
6. Present your show to your class. (Check with your teacher to arrange a time and day to perform.)

**Extension II:**                                  **TV Producer**
1. Produce your show on filmstrip.
2. Draw pictures on filmstrip that illustrate your show's story. Use colored pencils.
3. Record your show on the tape recorder. (You do the talking.)
4. Record sound effects or music, too.
5. Ask your teacher to check out the film projector.
6. Show your TV show to your class.

**Thinking Levels:**

Analysis, Synthesis

**Skills:**
- Demonstrates understanding of visual arts
- Creates original story
- Demonstrates correct use of various media to produce a film
- Produces an original TV show or film

# You Are a
# TV Producer

1. Make up a story. Be sure it has a beginning, middle, and an ending.

2. On the next page, draw and color five pictures that tell your story.

3. Cut the strips and paste them together.

4. Cut the TV on the cut lines.

5. Pull your strip through the slits as you tell and show your TV show to your class.

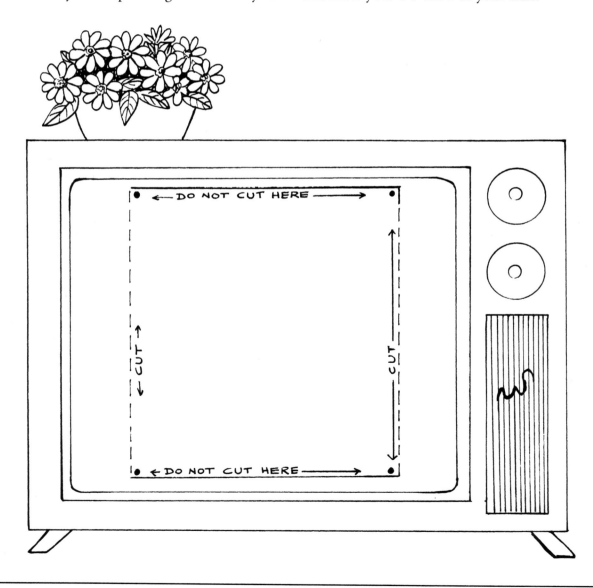

**Paste Here**

**Producer:**

**Title:**

**Paste Here**

# Language Arts

Autobiography • Bag Writing • Fairy Tales • Name Poems • Reading

The writing activities that follow are designed to help students enjoy the process of writing. Writing can help children see themselves and the world outside them more vividly, for writing makes them translate pictures or feelings into words. This translation of pictures and feelings into words uses Bloom's higher level thinking processes of analysis and synthesis.

The child may choose to handwrite or use a word processor to write the composition. Keep in mind that the creative-writing process the child experiences is more important than the final appearance of the product.

This section concludes with 32 ways children can share books with other students and a book cover if a child chooses to write a book report or an original book.

Louisa May Alcott was told by an editor that she could never write anything that had popular appeal.

**Basket Materials:**
- Autobiography Worksheets 1 & 2
- Writing paper
- Pencils
- Drawing paper
- Crayons or felt-tipped markers
- Glue

**Preparation:** Label basket *Autobiography* with blue tape. Photocopy 10 copies of each worksheet. Place in basket with other materials.

**Directions:** Copy the following on a white 4" x 6" note card, then laminate.

**Directions:**                              **Autobiography**
Instructions are on Writing an Autobiography Worksheet–1.

**Extension:** Copy the following on a blue 4" x 6" note card, then laminate.

**Extension:**                                **Autobiography**
1. After completing the first worksheet, you may want to make your own Autobiography Book.
2. If so, read the Autobiography Worksheet–2. Each part will be a chapter in your book. Print the title at the beginning of each chapter.
3. After you write a chapter, have the helper check it.
4. Don't forget to bring snapshots that fit with your chapters.
5. When you are done with all the chapters, you may want to type them on the computer or write them neatly.
6. The helper will bind them into a book for you. (See below.)

**Note to Teacher:** A short autobiography may be placed in the basket for the student to read before beginning this project so that the child understands that the author writes about him- or herself.

To make a book cover, have children bring in scraps of material (no less than 1/4 yard) at the beginning of the school year. Volunteers may glue or sew material onto a file folder. Insert completed autobiography into folder, punch with three-hole punch, and tie with yarn. This project is a beautiful keepsake!

**Thinking Levels:** Synthesis, Evaluation

**Skills:**
- Demonstrates understanding of an autobiography
- Creates and evaluates own autobiography
- Summarizes information
- Exercises writing skills

# Writing an Autobiography–1

Artists use paint, chalk, or crayons to draw pictures of themselves. Writers make self-portraits, too. They tell stories about themselves. Writers use pencils, paper, and words. You can make a self-portrait with words. Think about how you would finish these sentences.

My name is _____. I have _____ hair

and _____ eyes. I go to _____ School.

I am in the _____ grade. My teacher is _____.

In school, I like best to _____. At home, I

like to _____. My family members are

_____. I love to _____,

but I don't like to _____. My favorite food

is _____.

Write a paragraph about yourself. You can use some of the sentences above in your paragraph. Then, draw a self-portrait of yourself on drawing paper.

# Autobiography–2

1. Family History
   - Description of yourself.
   - Your birth (where, when, weight, length; anything unusual about your birth?).
   - Describe your family, including your pets.

2. Childhood Events
   - Name two important events that happened since you were born.
   - Write a separate paragraph for each event.

3. My First Day at School

4. What I Want to Be When I Grow Up and Why

5. My Favorite Teachers

6. My Favorite Vacation

7. My Best Effort

8. My Friends

9. My Favorite Poem

**Tips**
   - Each section should be on a separate sheet of paper.
   - Each section should be at least one paragraph.
   - Remember that a paragraph has at least three sentences.

**Color Code: Red**

**Basket Materials:**
- Bag full of miscellaneous objects
- Writing paper
- Drawing Paper
- Pencils
- Crayons or felt-tipped markers
- Colored pencils
- Tape recorder
- Blank tapes

**Preparation:** Label basket *Bag Writing* with red tape. Place materials in basket.

**Directions:** Copy the following on a white 4" x 6" note card, then laminate.

**Directions:**                                                    **Bag Writing**
1. Close your eyes and grab an object from the bag. Feel it without looking at it.
2. Place the object behind your back without looking at it.
3. Draw what you think the object is.
4. Look at the object and decide if you guessed right.
5. If you did not guess right, redraw the object.

**Extension:** Copy the following on blue 4" x 6" note cards, then laminate.

**Extension I:**                                                  **Bag Writing**
1. Close your eyes, put your hand in the bag, and grab a handful of objects.
2. Spread out the objects and think of a story that includes the objects you have picked from the bag. These items must be in the story.
3. Write a story and sketch the objects in the story. Design a cover page for your story.
4. The helper will bind your story.
5. Put your story in the library for others to read or share it with your class.

**Extension II:**                                                 **Bag Writing**
1. You can record a *movie* of your story.
2. Draw your story using only pictures to tell it.
3. Make up words to go with your pictures.
4. Record the story on a tape recorder. You may want to add music or sound effects.
5. Share your story with a class.

**Note to Teacher:** Magazine pictures or old photographs make great bag stuffers, too.

**Thinking Levels:**     Analysis, Synthesis

**Skills:**
- Synthesizes objects into a story
- Creates original story
- Demonstrates correct use of various media to produce a film
- Produces a film
- Exercises writing skills

**Basket Materials:**
- Short versions of fairy tales
- Fairy Tale Worksheet
- Tales Worksheet
- Writing paper
- Pencils
- Crayons or felt-tipped markers
- Plain, white paper
- Construction paper for covers
- Various materials for making puppets

**Preparation:**

Label basket *Fairy Tales* with red tape. Photocopy 10 copies of the Fairy Tales Worksheet on white paper and 10 copies of the Tales Worksheet on blue paper. Place materials in basket.

**Directions:**

Copy the following on a white 4" x 6" note card, then laminate.

**Directions:**                                          **Fairy Tales**
1. Take some time to read the fairy tales in the basket.
2. You will notice that most fairy tales have a setting (where the story takes place), characters (the people or creatures in the story), a problem, and a solution to the problem. In all fairy tales, some of the characters are good and some are evil.
3. After reading the fairy tales, pick one that you really like and fill out the Fairy Tale Worksheet using the fairy tale you picked.
4. Share it with your class.

**Extension:**

Copy the following on blue 4" x 6" note cards, then laminate.

**Extension I:**                                          **Fairy Tales**
1. Try your hand at writing your own fairy tale.
2. Take the Tales Worksheet (blue) and fill in the information on writing paper. This will be your title page.
3. Write your fairy tale.
4. Have the helper check it over and talk about things you might want to change before you do your final copy.
5. You may print or type your final copy. Include illustrations.
6. Design a cover for your story.
7. The helper will bind your story and cover.
8. Share your fairy tale with your class or the kindergarten classes.

**Extension II:**                                      **Fairy Tales**

1. Make puppets for a fairy tale that you make up. See the puppet basket for ideas for characters.
2. Color, cut, and paste the puppets.
3. Practice your puppet show for your class and ask for suggestions for improvement.
4. Share your puppet show with a kindergarten class. You may have friends help you.

**Thinking Levels:**            Analysis, Synthesis, Evaluation

**Skills:**
- Demonstrates understanding of the elements of a fairy tale
- Summarizes a fairy tale
- Writes, illustrates, and evaluates original fairy tale
- Creates, produces, and evaluates original puppet show
- Exercises writing skills

# Fairy Tales

1. Describe the characters (people in the story): _____
   _____
   _____
   _____

2. Add the setting (where the story takes place):_____
   _____
   _____
   _____

3. Explain the problem (the good and the evil in the fairy tale):_____
   _____
   _____
   _____

4. How is the problem solved (the solution to the evil)? _____
   _____
   _____
   _____

   <u>And they lived happily ever after!</u>

   **Title:** _____

   **Author:** _____

   **Name:** _____

# Tales

**Title:**

**Author:**

**Characters:**

**Setting:**

**Problem:**

**Solution:**

**Basket Materials:**
- Name Poem Worksheet
- Pencils
- Crayons or felt-tipped markers
- Poster board
- Scraps of colored construction paper
- Paper
- Glue

**Preparation:** Label basket *Name Poems* with red tape. Photocopy 10 copies of the Name Poem Worksheet and place in basket along with other materials.

**Directions:** Copy the following on a white 4" x 6" note card, then laminate.

**Directions:**                                    **Name Poems**
Instructions are included on the worksheet.

**Extension:** Copy the following on a blue 4" x 6" note card, then laminate.

**Extension:**                                    **Name Poems**
1. Think of a creative way to design a poster board with your name on it.
   **or**
2. Illustrate your Name Poem.
3. Display your creation in your classroom.

**Thinking Levels:** Analysis, Synthesis

**Skills:**
- Demonstrates understanding of an adjective
- Exercises reference skills and use of the dictionary
- Increases vocabulary
- Creates original Name Poem

# Name Poem

A poem tells about a person. Each line of a name poem is an adjective.

**Here is an example for Brian.**

**B** <u>ossy</u> _____
**R** <u>ich</u> _____
**I** <u>ntelligent</u> _____
**A** <u>ctive</u> _____
**N** <u>ice</u> _____

**Think of words for Fred.**

**F** _____
**R** _____
**E** _____
**D** _____

**Write a name poem for yourself.**
(You may use a dictionary).

_____
_____
_____
_____
_____
_____
_____
_____
_____
_____
_____

**Write a name poem for a friend.**
(You may give it to her/him.)

_____
_____
_____
_____
_____
_____
_____
_____
_____
_____
_____

Can you think of a name poem for your teacher or your principal?

**Basket Materials:**
- Any books that are above grade level
- List of ideas as follows
- Access to various materials

**Preparation:**

Label basket *Reading* with red tape. Put in various books that are above grade level.

Photocopy the 32 ways to share a book on blue paper, then laminate entire list. Another idea: Type each of the 32 ways to share a book on separate 4" x 6" blue note cards and attach all to a key chain.

**Directions:**

Copy the following on a white 4" x 6" note card, then laminate.

**Directions:**                                                    **Reading**
1. Select a book to read.

**Extension:**

After you have finished reading a book, choose one of the following ideas to share your book with others:

**Extensions:**                                                   **Reading**
1. Make a poster to advertise your book. Use paint, crayons, chalk, or whatever you can find to create your poster. Make a flat or a three-dimensional poster.
2. Decorate a book jacket for your book and write an advertisement to go with it.
3. Write a book review for the school newspaper.
4. Create a series of original illustrations for your story using any medium (paint, crayons, chalk, etc.).
5. Give a dramatization with other children who are reading the same book. You may dress up in costumes.
6. Write a different ending for the story you read.
7. Tell the story to a musical accompaniment of your choice.
8. Write a letter to a friend to recommend your book.
9. Prepare a puppet show to illustrate your story. See the Puppet basket for ideas for puppets.
10. Broadcast a book review to an imaginary radio audience. Include background music and sound effects.
11. Dress as one of the characters in the book and tell the story from his or her point of view.
12. Find out about the author and present a brief biography. Include sketches of the author's books.
13. Make a face mask of a character in your story and tell about him or her.

14. Make flannel cutouts of the main characters and tell your story with flannelgraph. (Have your teacher get a flannelgraph board.)

15. Make paper-stuffed characters and tell the story. Draw characters double, stuff with tissue paper or newspaper, staple together, glue onto popsicle sticks.

16. Illustrate five main events of the book on poster board.

17. Create an interview with the main character. You could be a reporter for a television station or a newspaper. Use a tape recorder and play both parts or have a friend interview you as you pretend to be the main character.

18. Create a diorama in a shoe box showing your favorite scene or setting.

19. Design awards to be given to the characters in the book. Think of their special talents and create ribbons or trophies to award them.

20. Paint a mural of your favorite scene or design it to show the entire story.

21. Write a letter to the main character in the book. Ask questions you've been wondering about since you've finished reading it.

22. Write a song about the book.

23. Write to the author of the book.

24. Create a mobile of scenes from the book.

25. Give a step-by-step demonstration of something you learned from reading the book.

26. Write a poem about your favorite character from the book.

27. Develop a newspaper headline, picture, and article describing the major events in the book.

28. Create a bookmark that best describes the book you have read.

29. Use colored chalk to draw a picture on the blackboard while you are telling the story to the class. This is called "chalk talk."

30. Design and put up a bulletin board of several books your favorite author has written or about several of your favorite books on the same subject.

31. Think of your own way to share your book.

32. Write your own book. You can use the Light Bright Book Cover for your cover page or design your own.

There are so many ways to share books! Put a cozy pillow at the Light Bright Center and let students read until their hearts' content. Remind them that they must share the book in some way.

# Light
## Bright
## Book Cover

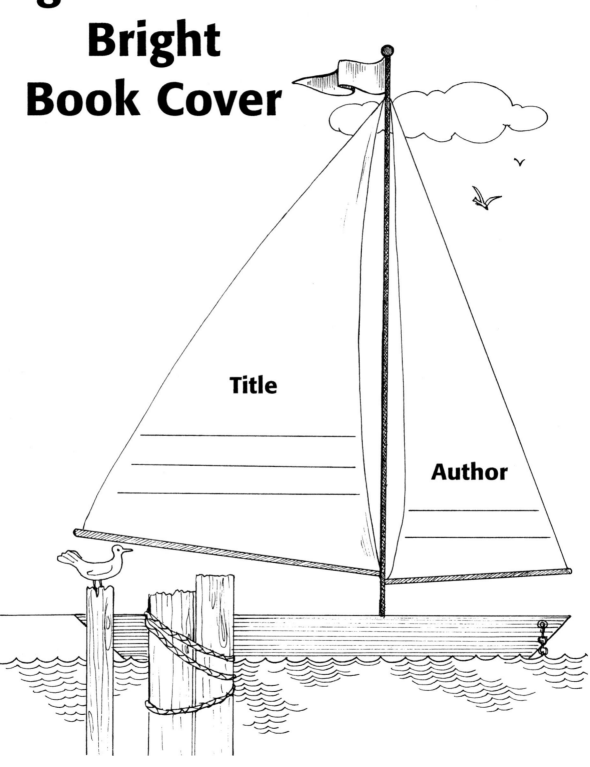

Title

_____

_____

_____

Author

_____

_____

# Mathematics

Birthday Cake Math • Toothpick Towers • Pizza Math • Tangrams

Math materials for baskets should promote problem-solving skills, student creativity, and critical thinking skills. These skills teach children how to think and are precisely the skills emphasized with gifted and talented students.

Light Bright math materials should not be repetitive worksheets done in the classroom or worksheets that ask the child merely to recall numbers and facts. The goal of Light Bright math baskets is to provide children an opportunity to apply their math knowledge to higher level thinking and problem-solving activities. A variety of manipulatives should be included in math baskets, and the activities should be fun and promote problem-solving skills.

Enclosed in this section are a few sample math activities that give one an idea of what math basket projects should be like.

Einstein was four years old
before he could speak and
seven before he could read.

| | |
|---|---|
| **Basket Materials:** | • Birthday Cake Worksheet<br>• Pencils<br>• Rulers |
| **Preparation:** | Label basket *Birthday Cake Math* with red tape. Photocopy 10 copies of the Birthday Cake Worksheet. Place materials in basket. |
| **Directions:** | Copy the following on a white 4" x 6" note card, then laminate. |

**Directions:**　　　　　　　　　　　　**Birthday Cake Math**

Instructions are on the worksheet.

| | |
|---|---|
| **Extension:** | Copy the following on a blue 4" x 6" note card, then laminate. |

**Extension:**　　　　　　　　　　　　**Birthday Cake Math**

1. Ask your parents for permission to make two cakes for your class.
2. Bring the uncut cakes to school.
3. You will probably have more than 16 children in your class. You have to cut the cake so that each child in your class gets the same-sized piece.
4. Serve and enjoy!

| | |
|---|---|
| **Thinking Levels:** | Analysis, Synthesis |
| **Skills:** | • Demonstrates understanding of equal parts<br>• Analyzes information<br>• Demonstrates the understanding of the mathematical operation of division<br>• Synthesizes information<br>• Exercises problem-solving skills |

# Birthday Cakes

You are at a birthday party. There are 16 children at the party including yourself. There are two square birthday cakes and both are the same size. Each child wants a piece of cake exactly the same size. You are asked to cut the birthday cakes.

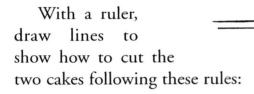

With a ruler, draw lines to show how to cut the two cakes following these rules:

1. You must cut straight lines.

2. Each piece has to be exactly the same size.

3. You must cut each cake differently!

**Hint:** First, determine how many pieces there will be on each cake.

## Possible Solutions—Birthday Cake Math

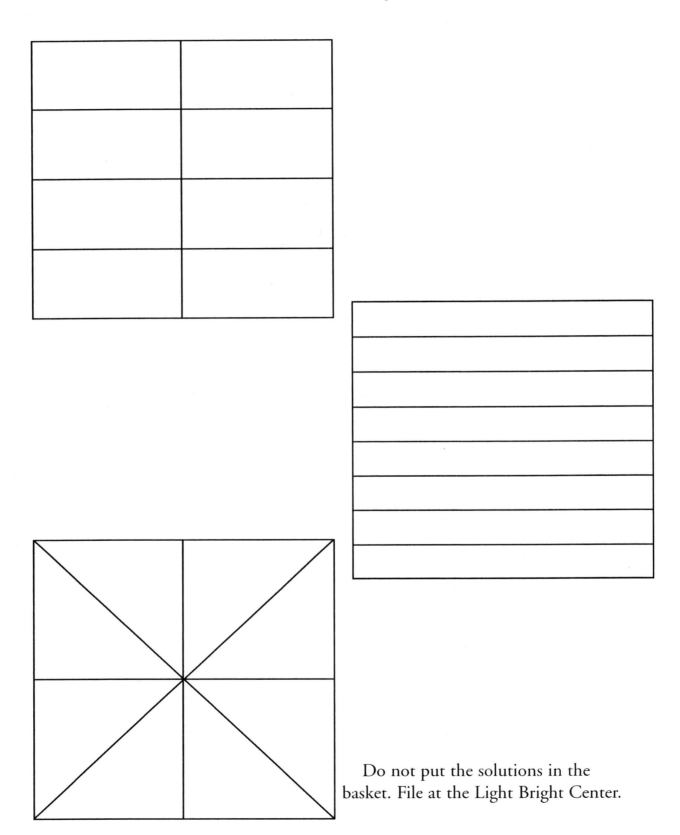

Do not put the solutions in the
basket. File at the Light Bright Center.

**Basket Materials:**

- Toothpick Towers Worksheet
- Toothpicks
- Styrofoam® packing pieces
- Pencils
- Rulers
- Writing Paper
- Drawing Paper
- Access to a camera

**Preparation:**

Label basket *Toothpick Towers* with blue tape. Photocopy about 10 copies of the worksheet and place in basket with other materials.

**Directions:**

Copy the following on a white 4" x 6" note card, then laminate.

**Directions:**          **Toothpick Towers**

1. Take 15 toothpicks and 15 Styrofoam® pieces.
2. Build the tallest tower you can using all of the toothpicks and Styrofoam® pieces. The tower must stand alone without falling.
3. When you are finished, measure the height of the tower.
4. Record your name, date, and height of your Toothpick Tower on the Recording Worksheet in the basket.
5. You might want to save your Toothpick Tower for a blue card activity.

**Extension:**

Copy the following on blue 4" x 6" note cards, then laminate.

**Extension I:**          **Toothpick Towers**

1. Take a photograph of your Toothpick Tower or draw it.
2. Write a real estate advertisement for the newspaper in which you will try to sell your Toothpick Tower to potential buyers.

**or**

3. Design a newspaper ad that will attract tourists to your Toothpick Tower.
4. Display your Toothpick Tower and ad in the library or at a real estate office

**Extension II:**          **Toothpick Towers**

1. Using toothpicks and Styrofoam® pieces, create an original invention that will be useful to humankind in the future.
2. Give your invention a name.
3. Write about your invention: what it is, how it was constructed, and how it will be useful to humankind in the future.
4. Share your invention with your class or display at a science fair.

**Thinking Levels:**

Analysis, Synthesis, Evaluation

**Color Code: Red**

**Skills:**

- Evaluates the relevancy of data
- Analyzes information
- Demonstrates understanding of geometric design
- Exercises problem-solving skills
- Creates original invention

# Toothpick Towers

| Recording–Toothpick Towers | | | | | |
|---|---|---|---|---|---|
| **Name** | **Date** | **Height** | **Name** | **Date** | **Height** |
| | | | | | |
| | | | | | |
| | | | | | |
| | | | | | |
| | | | | | |
| | | | | | |
| | | | | | |
| | | | | | |

| | |
|---|---|
| **Basket Materials:** | • Pizza Worksheet<br>• Pencils<br>• Rulers<br>• Pizza recipe |
| **Preparation:** | Label basket *Pizza Math* with red tape. Photocopy 10 copies each of the Pizza Worksheet and the pizza recipe and place in the basket with the other materials. |
| **Directions:** | Copy the following on a blue 4" x 6" note card, then laminate. |

**Directions:**                                                    **Pizza Math**
Instructions are on the worksheet.

| | |
|---|---|
| **Extension:** | Copy the following on a white 4" x 6" note card, then laminate. |

**Extension:**                                                    **Pizza Math**
1. Help make a pizza at home. Take a copy of the pizza recipe.
2. Cut the pizza the way you did on your worksheet. Did it work?
3. Have your parents write a note stating that you completed this project.

| | |
|---|---|
| **Thinking Levels:** | Analysis, Synthesis |
| **Skills:** | • Analyzes information<br>• Synthesizes information<br>• Exercises problem-solving skills |

# Pizza Math

You and your family are at a pizza restaurant. You have seven people in your family including yourself. Draw lines with a ruler to show how you should cut the pizza following these rules:

1.  Each person only gets one piece of pizza.

2.  You can use only three straight lines.

**Hint:** The pieces do not have to be the same size.

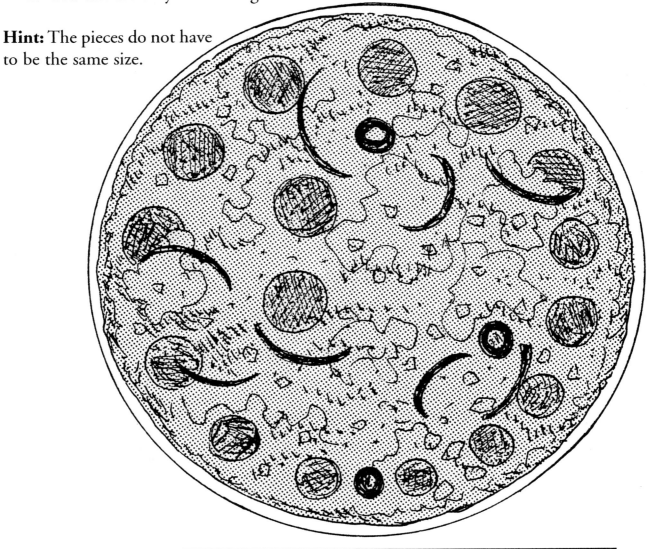

# Pizza Math

## Solution

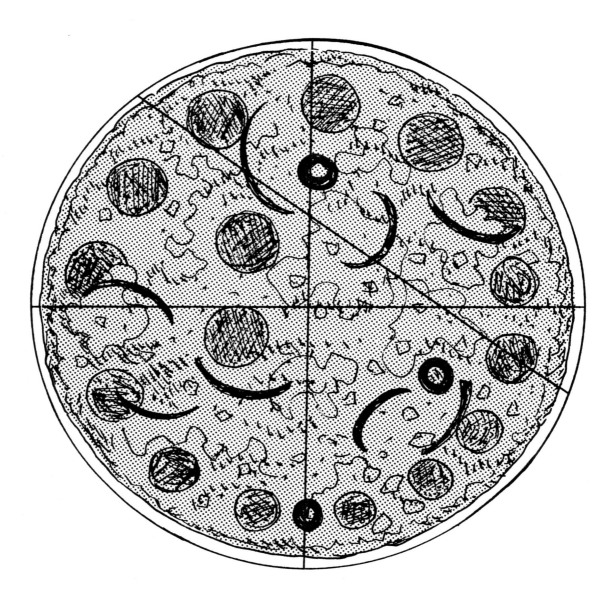

Do not put the solutions in the  basket. File at the Light Bright Center.

# Pepperoni Pizza Recipe

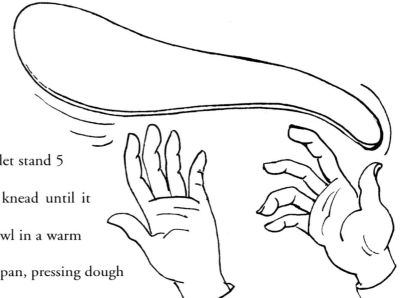

**Crust:**
½ cup warm (105°–115°) water
1 package dry yeast
1½ cups flour
½ teaspoon salt
1 tablespoon cooking oil

1. Dissolve the yeast in water and let stand 5 minutes.
2. Stir in flour, salt, and oil and knead until it forms a smooth ball.
3. Let rise in a greased, covered bowl in a warm place (80°) until doubled.
4. Pat dough on greased 12" pizza pan, pressing dough up the sides.

**Filling:**
1 6 oz. can tomato paste
1 teaspoon garlic salt
½ teaspoon oregano
¼ teaspoon cayenne pepper

1. Mix tomato paste and sauce in bowl.
2. Add garlic salt, oregano, and cayenne pepper. Mix well.
3. Spread over crust.

½ cup chopped onion
½ cup sliced, black olives
½ cup sliced, fresh mushrooms
½ pound grated mozzarella cheese
½ pound sliced pepperoni

1. Sprinkle the cheese evenly over the filling.
2. Top with onions, olives, mushrooms, and pepperoni.
3. Dot with butter or margarine.
4. Bake 400°F or 30–35 minutes.

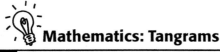

**Basket Materials:**
- 2 sets of Tangrams in envelopes made with seven geometric pieces:
  - Five triangles (two small, one medium, and two large)
  - one Rhomboid
  - one Square
- Envelopes
- Puzzle Worksheets
- The *Fun With Tangrams Kit* (Johnston, 1977) or any tangram kit found in a bookstore
- Pencils
- Paper

**Preparation:**

Label basket *Tangrams* with red tape. Photocopy the two sets of tangram pieces on tagboard, cut, then laminate. Put each set into an envelope and mark the pieces on the front of the envelope. Place materials in basket along with any tangram kit or the one suggested above. Photocopy Puzzle Worksheets on tagboard, then laminate. Place in the basket.

**Directions:**

Copy the following on a white 4" x 6" note card, then laminate.

**Directions:**                                                        **Tangrams**
1. Try to arrange the tangram pieces so they will fit into the figures on the tangram worksheets.
2. They must fit tightly together and may not overlap. You cannot cut them.
3. Try to do as many worksheets as you can.

**Extension:**

To be used with Susan Johnston's *Fun With Tangrams Kit*.

Copy the following on a blue 4" x 6" note card, then laminate.

**Extension:**                                                        **Tangrams**
1. Explore the tangram book.
2. The trick is to arrange the pieces to form the silhouettes of the people, animals, and objects that are printed on the pages in the book. You must use all seven tangram pieces.
3. You can also use the tangram pieces to form your own tangrams, but you must use all seven pieces.
4. Create your own tangram worksheet, put your name on it, and have the helper laminate it for you. You may place it in the Tangram Basket.

Note to Teacher:

Steps 3 and 4 can be used for Extension without purchasing *Fun with Tangrams Kit*.

**Thinking Levels:**     Analysis, Synthesis

**Skills:**
- Exercises problem-solving skills
- Creates original tangram
- Summarizes data

# Two Sets of Tangrams

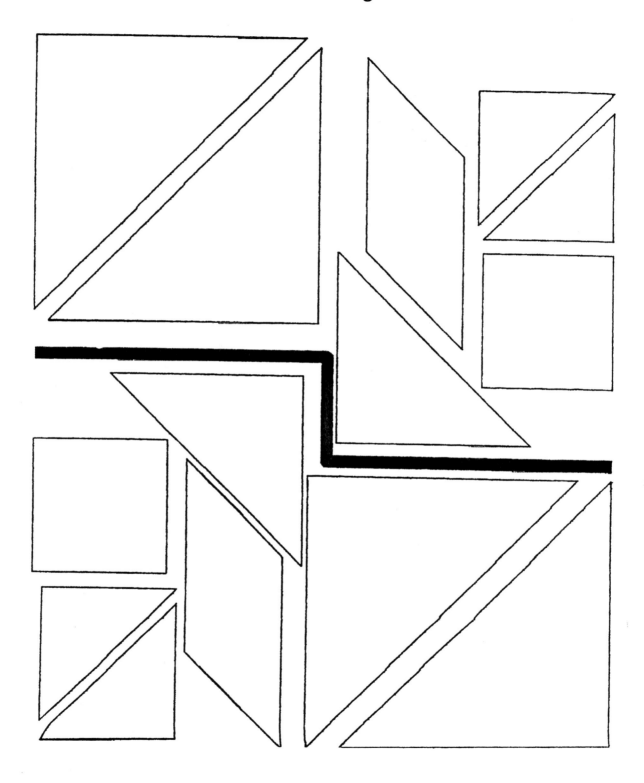

# Tangram Puzzle—1

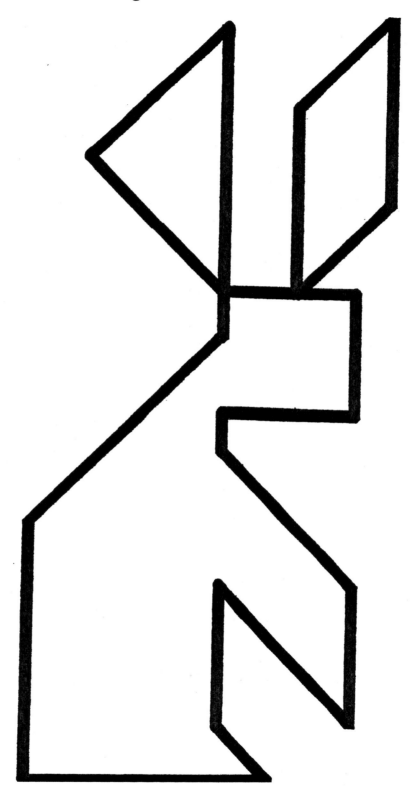

# Tangram Puzzle—3

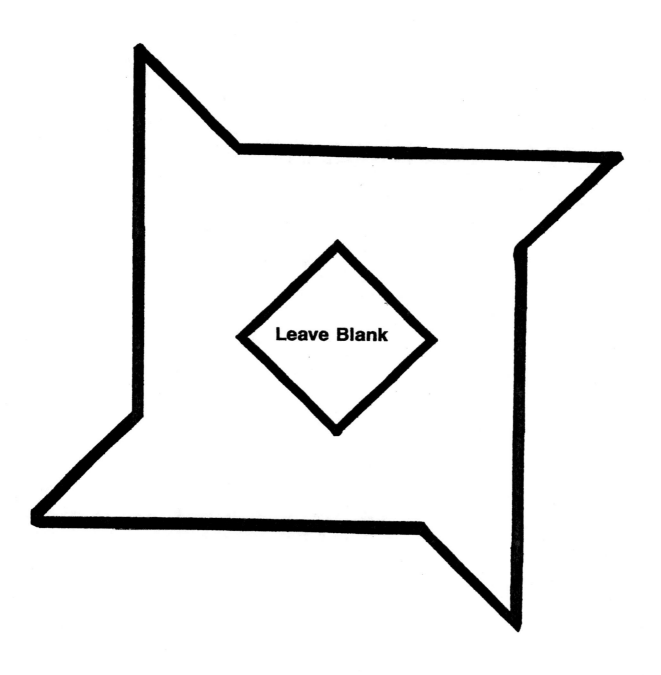

Leave Blank

# Tangram Puzzles—Solutions

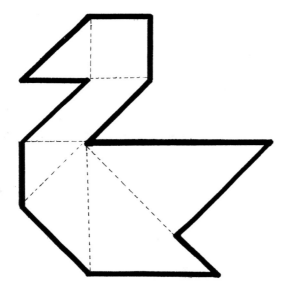

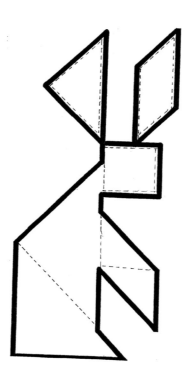

Do not put solutions in basket. File at the Light Bright Center.

# Tangram Puzzles—Solutions

Leave Blank

Do not put solutions in basket. File at the Light Bright Center.

# Research, Inventions, and Games

Checkers • Game Inventions • Inventions • Research

Students who learn library and research procedures—finding reference materials, using the card catalog, compiling a bibliography—will have valuable learning tools that they can use all of their lives. Topics for research baskets are endless. Often, a student will want to research a subject that may not be included in the basket. Please encourage students to do so. Inventions are included in this section because they involve research skills, as well. Suggestions included here are ideas to get you started in compiling your research and invention baskets, ideas for book games, and board games that require strategy and higher level thinking skills.

When Thomas Edison was a boy,
his teachers told him he was
too stupid to learn anything.

| | |
|---|---|
| **Basket Materials:** | • Checker board<br>• Set of checkers |
| **Preparation:** | Label basket *Checkers* with blue tape. Laminate the directions to the checker game. Place directions in basket with game set. |
| **Directions:** | Directions for playing Checkers are in the basket. (Laminate original game rules.) |
| **Extension:** | Put the extension activities in a separate basket. |
| **Other Games for Baskets:** | • Battleship®<br>• Chess<br>• Chinese Checkers®<br>• Pente® |
| **Note to Teacher:** | Watch carefully that the same students don't do this basket over and over. If they do, instruct them to move on to a blue task card activity (Extensions). |
| **Thinking Levels:** | Synthesis, Evaluation |
| **Skills:** | • Exercises problem-solving skills<br>• Develops strategies<br>• Predicts outcomes<br>• Infers information |

**Color Code: Blue**

**Basket Materials:**

- Sketching paper
- Pencils
- Erasers
- Crayons or felt-tipped markers
- Glue
- Scissors
- Writing paper
- Cardboard scraps or poster board
- 3" x 5" index cards (various colors) or paper (for direction game cards)
- Bag of various objects

**Preparation:**

Label basket *Game Inventions* with blue tape. Place materials in basket along with a bag of objects that could be used as game markers: buttons, bottle caps, pennies, shells, paper clips, dried beans, and so forth. You may want to purchase a quantity of dice or have the students purchase their own.

**Extension:**

Copy the following on blue 4" x 6" note cards, then laminate.

**Extension I:**                                                                            **Games**

1. Think of an idea for a game.
2. Determine the goal of the game—how does a player win the game?
3. Establish a way to start and finish your game.
4. Decide on some obstacles/problems that will set players back and successes that will move players ahead. Write these on the index cards. The advances will be on one color. The obstacles will be on a different color.
5. Design your game on paper first.
6. Write the rules to the game on writing paper.
7. Decide which markers you will use.
8. Play your game with someone else to determine what needs improving and adjusting.
9. Have your partner help you evaluate your game.
10. Carefully copy your game onto cardboard or poster board. Your teacher will laminate the game board after you have colored it.

**Extension II:**                                **Games**

1. Instead of thinking of any idea for a game, your game must be based on a book that you have recently read.
2. The characters in the book will be your markers.
3. How the book begins and ends will be the start and finish to your game.
4. The problems the characters encounter in the book will be the obstacles in the game.
5. How the characters overcome their problems in the book will be the advances in the game.
6. The plot of the book will be the design for the game board.
7. Play the game before you make your final copy. Determine if you need to make changes.
8. Make your final copy.
9. You have just invented a book game!

**Note to teacher:**     This is a great project to do with your highest ability reading group.

**Thinking Levels:**     Analysis, Synthesis, Evaluation

**Skills:**

• Demonstrates understanding of the elements of a game
• Analyzes, relates, and summarizes information
• Exercises problem-solving skills and strategy skills
• Creates original invention
• Evaluates information and outcomes

**Color Code: Blue**

| | |
|---|---|
| **Basket Materials:** | • Invent a Machine Worksheet<br>• Machine Parts Worksheet<br>• Grade-level reading books about inventors<br>• Scissors<br>• Glue<br>• Pencils<br>• Crayons or felt-tipped markers<br>• Drawing paper<br>• Box lids and box of junk |

**Preparation:** Label basket *Inventions* with blue tape. Photocopy 10 copies each of the Invent a Machine Worksheets. Place in the basket with the other materials.

**Directions:** Copy the following on a white 4" x 6" white note card, then laminate.

**Directions:**                                     **Inventions**
1. Take the Invent a Machine Worksheets and follow the directions.
2. Share your invention with your class.

**Extension:** Copy the following on blue 4" x 6" note cards, then laminate.

**Extension I:**                                     **Inventions**
1. The Ferris Wheel is a kind of wheel found in amusement parks.
2. Invent a new ride for an amusement park.
3. Design your ride on paper first. Label the parts and explain how it works. Give your ride a name.
4. Build a real model of your new ride.
5. Get together with other students who have built new rides and build a new kind of amusement park.

**Extension II:**                                     **Inventions**
1. Build a machine of the future using only junk. Decide what junk you will use.
2. Design your junk machine on paper first.
3. Gather your junk and build it using tape to hold the parts together. Build it in a box lid.
4. Display your junk machine at the science fair.

**Other Ways to share:** Have an Inventor's Week so you can display inventions and give awards for the most original, most useful, most complicated inventions, and so forth.

**Thinking Levels:** Analysis, Synthesis, Evaluation

**Skills:**

- Analyzes and summarizes information
- Creates and tests new ideas
- Exercises problem-solving skills
- Evaluates feasibility of invention
- Designs and creates original model

# Invent a Machine

Machines and robots help us to do jobs faster!

Directions:

1. Decide on a machine that you would like to invent and what it will do.

2. On a piece of paper, draw a large square, a circle, or a triangle.

3. Cut out any of the parts on the next page and glue them onto the shape you have drawn to make your machine or robot.

4. Name your machine or robot: _____
   _____

5. What does it do for you? _____
   _____

6. How does it work? _____
   _____

7. Share your invention with your class.

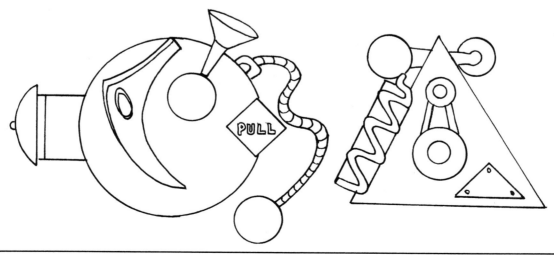

# Machine Parts

PUSH

PULL

**Basket Materials:**
- Research Cards
- Writing paper
- Pencils
- Construction paper for covers
- Bibliography

**Preparation:** Label basket *Research* with blue tape. On 4" x 6" white note cards, write a separate research topic on each, such as dinosaurs, insects, transportation of the future, moon, and so forth. Laminate them, place the white directions note card on top, and attach all to a key ring. Place in basket. You could brainstorm with your class about topics that are interesting to them. Include topics that complement your curriculum.

**Directions:** Copy the following on a white 4" x 6" white note card, then laminate.

**Directions:**                                   **Research**
1. Pick a research card that looks interesting to you—select something you'd like to know more about.
2. You may take a library pass and do your research at the library quietly. Spend about 30 minutes there.
3. Show the Light Bright helper what you've written each time you go to the library.
4. Compile your research into a report.
5. Make a cover for your report.
6. Complete the bibliography that lists your sources.
7. Share your report with your class.

**Extension:** Copy the following on a blue 4" x 6" note card, then laminate

**Extension:**                                    **Research**
1. Make one or more visual aides to go with your report. Some ideas are: bulletin board, model, display, mural, poster, Light Bright basket, maps/charts, diorama, mobile, table display, collage, slide show, or come up with your own idea. It's your chance to be creative!
2, Sign up for Kids Teaching Day so that you can share your creation with your class.

**Thinking Levels:** Synthesis, Evaluation

**Skills:**
- Exercises research skills
- Summarizes and evaluates information
- Understands and completes a bibliography
- Creates original report and visual aid

# Report

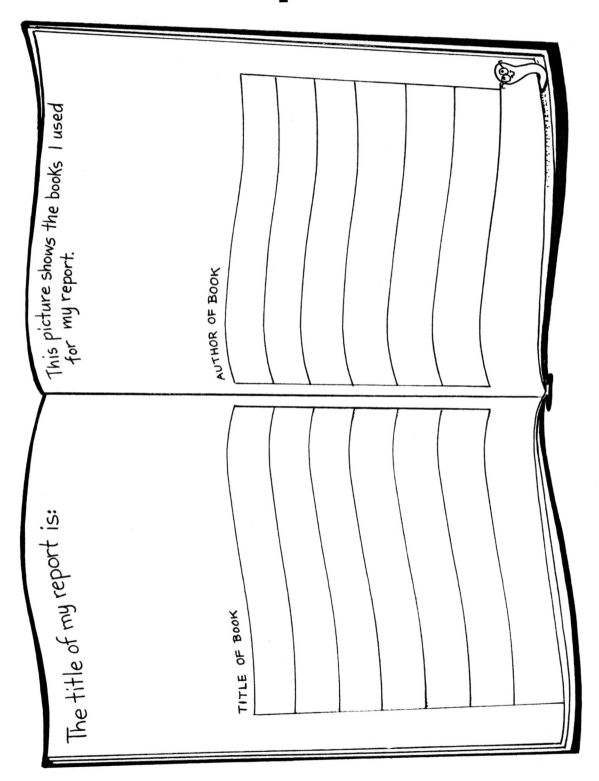

This picture shows the books I used for my report.

AUTHOR OF BOOK

The title of my report is:

TITLE OF BOOK

# Science

Airplanes • Birds • Crystal Garden • Liquids • Weather

The science activities presented here focus on science as a problem-solving process. Used in this manner, the process uses creativity perhaps even more than intelligence. Some science baskets contain a short science experiment that allows students to investigate scientific concepts about our world. Truth becomes real to children when they observe and find out for themselves, not because someone else says so. Young children hunger for truth. They want to know how and why things work. Their curiosity is never ending.

Light Bright science baskets provide an opportunity for children to investigate on their own or with a partner. The students test information and draw conclusions on their own. The Light Bright volunteer serves as a guide, not as the implementer.

Science resources for science basket materials are endless. Also consider the problem-solving section in your science text, higher grade science materials, *National Geographic* kits, or any other science kits in your school.

**Isaac Newton did poorly
in grade school.**

**Basket Materials:**
- *The Paper Airplane Book* (Simon, 1987), or any book that demonstrates the principles of flying
- Airplane Materials Worksheet
- 8½ x 11 construction paper or drawing paper
- Scissors
- Paper clips
- Rulers
- Crayons or felt-tipped markers
- Transparent tape
- Pencils
- Straws
- Scraps of tagboard
- Writing paper

**Preparation:**
Label basket *Airplanes* with blue tape. Place *The Paper Airplane Book* in the basket along with the other materials. Photocopy 10 copies of the worksheet and place in the basket.

**Note to teacher:**
The tasks in this basket will take many sessions, even the white note card.

**Directions:**
Copy the following on a white 4" x 6" white note card, then laminate.

**Directions:**                                                    **Airplanes**
1. Read *The Paper Airplane Book* in the basket.
2. Try some or all of the experiments in the book. These experiments teach you about how and why airplanes fly.
3. You may fly paper airplanes on the playground for experiments.
4. Write down what you learned about how airplanes fly.

**Extension:**
Copy the following on blue 4" x 6" note cards, then laminate.

**Extension I:**                                                   **Airplanes**
1. Get together with other students who have also made paper airplanes. Organize a paper plane flying contest on the playground.
2. Choose different categories—the fastest, highest, lowest, most creative, and so forth.
3. Try putting paper clips on different parts of the plane. See if weighting the plane in different parts makes it go higher, lower, slower, or faster. Design a chart to record your results.
4. After the contest, discuss the results with your class. Show and explain your chart on the blackboard.

**Extension II:**                                                    **Airplanes**

1. You are now ready to build an original aircraft that you have drawn.
2. List the materials you will need on the Airplane Materials Worksheet. Ask your parents and friends for materials.
3. Assemble and label your aircraft.
4. Decorate your aircraft with materials from the basket.
5. Demonstrate how your model works to your class.

**Thinking Levels:**          Application, Analysis, Synthesis, Evaluation

**Skills:**

- Demonstrates understanding of basic concepts of aeronautics
- Develops and organizes a contest
- Categorizes and records information
- Records, interprets, and summarizes data
- Justifies and applies conclusions
- Exercises research skills
- Demonstrates leadership skills

# Airplane Materials

_____

_____

_____

_____

_____

_____

_____

_____

_____

_____

_____

_____

_____

_____

_____

**Color Code: Red**

| | |
|---|---|
| **Basket Materials:** | • Bag of yarn scraps, string, wood shavings, straw, twigs, moss, etc. |
| | • Bird books with pictures of nests and habitats |
| | • Writing paper |
| | • Pencils |
| | • 4" x 6" index cards |
| | • Bird Worksheet |
| | • Bibliography page |

**Preparation:** Label basket *Birds* with red tape. Photocopy 10 copies of Bird Worksheet and the Bibliography page. Place in basket along with other materials.

**Directions:** Copy the following on a white 4" x 6" white note card, then laminate.

**Directions:**                                                                   **Birds**
1. Take some time to look through the bird books and observe different kinds of birds' nests.
2. Choose the kind of nest you would like to make. It must be a nest of a bird whose habitat is in your region. Define habitat on paper. You may use a dictionary.
3. Use the materials that an animal might find in its habitat to make a nest. Remember—a bird does not have glue.
4. Very carefully, place your finished nest on the science table in your classroom.
5. Take an index card and write your name and the date. Write the kind of bird that lives in the nest you made and describe its habitat. Place the card by the nest.

**Extension:** Copy the following on blue 4" x 6" note cards, then laminate.

**Extension I:**                                                                  **Birds**
1. Go to the library quietly and do some research on birds.
2. Decide which bird you would like to do a report on.
3. Collect all the information you can about the bird you have selected. Fill in the Bibliography page.
4. Fill in the answers on the Birds Worksheet.
5. Put your report together and make a cover.
6. Draw your bird.
7. Bind your report and cover into a book.

**Extension II:**                                             **Birds**

1. Construct a diorama of a bird and its habitat that you have studied.
   - **Diorama** is a three-dimensional miniature scene with model figures and a painted background that looks real.
   - **Habitat** is the place where the bird is mostly found, lives, and raises its young.
2. Use a shoe box for your diorama. Paint the shoe box on the inside to look like the bird's habitat.
3. You can use real grass, moss, twigs, hay, and tree branches.
4. Make paper birds.
5. After the paint is dry and you have gathered all of your materials, carefully glue them in place inside the shoe box.
6. Label your diorama, include the name of the bird, and briefly write about its habitat.

**Thinking Levels:**           Analysis, Synthesis,

**Skills:**
- Applies principles of building a bird's nest
- Demonstrates understanding of the concept of habitat, diorama
- Analyzes and summarizes information into a report
- Demonstrates understanding of a bibliography

# Birds Worksheet

1. Here are some facts about _____

2. This bird lives _____

3. It eats _____

4. It raises its young _____

5. Materials it uses to build its nest are _____

6. Its habitat is _____

7. It preys on _____

8. Its predators are _____

9. It migrates _____

10. This bird can (anything unusual) _____
    _____
    _____

Add anything else you think is important. Draw and color the bird for the cover to your report. Give your report a title.

YOU'RE BRIGHT

# Birds Report

This picture shows the books I used for my report.

AUTHOR OF BOOK

The title of my report is:

TITLE OF BOOK

**Basket Materials:**
- Torn sponge
- Medium glass bowl
- Tablespoon
- Bluing
- Ammonia
- Salt
- Food coloring
- Eye dropper
- Plastic bowl
- Spoon for mixing

**Preparation:** Label basket *Crystal Garden* with red tape. Place materials in the basket.

**Directions:** Copy the following on a white 4" x 6" white note card, then laminate.

**Directions:**                                           **Crystal Garden**
1. Soak the sponge until it is very wet.
2. Drain. Place it in a glass bowl.
3. Mix a solution of:
   - 4 tablespoons water
   - 4 tablespoons bluing
   - 4 tablespoons ammonia
   - A few drops of food coloring.
4. Pour solution over sponge in glass bowl.
5. Sprinkle salt all over the sponge.
6. In two or three days, you should have a crystal garden.
7. When your crystal garden begins to dry, add 2 tablespoons water and 2 tablespoons ammonia.

**Extension:** Copy the following on a blue 4" x 6" note card, then laminate.

**Extension:**                                          **Crystal Garden**
1. Sign up for a Kids Teaching Day. Demonstrate how to make a crystal garden to a class.
2. Write down on a piece of paper why the crystal garden grew from the ingredients you used. You may have to go to the library and do some research.
3. Explain to your class the way crystal garden grows.
4. You may want to hand out the recipe for crystal gardens to your classmates.

**Thinking Levels:** Analysis, Synthesis

**Skills:**

- Applies and summarizes information
- Demonstrates a scientific experiment
- Explains scientific concepts
- Exercises research skills
- Demonstrates leadership skills

| | |
|---|---|
| **Basket Materials:** | • Eye droppers<br>• Dish detergent<br>• Oil<br>• Water<br>• Tablespoons<br>• Screw-top glass jars<br>• Liquids Worksheet<br>• Writing paper<br>• Pencils |
| **Preparation:** | Label basket *Liquids* with blue tape. Photocopy 10 copies of the Liquids Worksheet and place in basket along with other materials. Place dish detergent, oil, and water in separate jars with lids. |
| **Directions:** | Copy the following on a white 4" x 6" white not card, then laminate. |

**Directions**                                                    **Liquids**
1. Measure 5 tablespoons of cooking oil and 5 tablespoons of water into the jar.
2. Screw on the lid and vigorously shake the jar.
3. What happens to the liquids?
4. Leave the jar for a minute. What happens to the liquids? Why?
5. Using an eye dropper, add about 10 drops of dish detergent to the jar. Shake the jar. What happens? Why?

| | |
|---|---|
| **Extension:** | Copy the following on a blue 4" x 6" note card, then laminate. |

**Extension:**                                                    **Liquids**
1. After you did the experiment on the white note card, you actually discovered what happens during an oil spill in the ocean.
2. Find a way to clean up the ocean water and dispose of the oil in a way that is safe to the environment.
3. You may have to do some research.
4. Write down your solution, draw a diagram of your solution, or make a model of your solution.

| | |
|---|---|
| **Thinking Levels:** | Analysis, Synthesis, Evaluation |
| **Skills:** | • Demonstrates understanding of the scientific concept of emulsion<br>• Distinguishes differences<br>• Compares, summarizes, and evaluates information<br>• Develops and applies conclusions<br>• Creates original invention/solution |

# Liquids

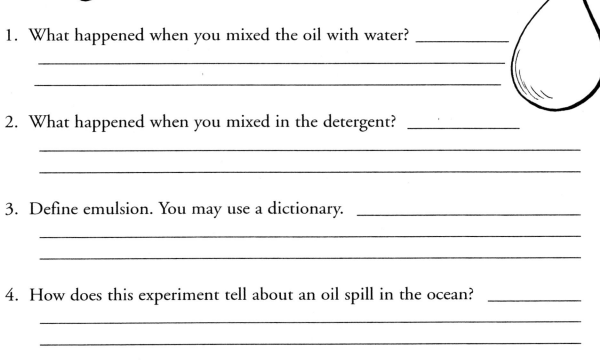

1. What happened when you mixed the oil with water? _____
   _____
   _____

2. What happened when you mixed in the detergent? _____
   _____
   _____

3. Define emulsion. You may use a dictionary. _____
   _____
   _____

4. How does this experiment tell about an oil spill in the ocean? _____
   _____
   _____
   _____

| | |
|---|---|
| **Basket Materials:** | • Weather Worksheets |
| | • Books about weather and weather predictions |
| | • Pencils |
| | • Old magazines |
| | • Writing paper |
| | • Scissors |
| | • Construction paper for scrap book cover |
| | • Glue |
| | • Current weather report |

**Preparation:**  Label basket *Weather* with blue tape. Make about 10 copies of the worksheets. Staple the Weather Station Worksheets together. Place in basket along with other materials.

**Directions:**  Copy the following on a white 4" x 6" note card, then laminate.

**Directions:**                                        **Weather**
Take out the Weather Worksheet and fill in the answers.

**Extensions:**  Copy the following on blue 4" x 6" note cards, then laminate.

**Extension I:**                                        **Weather**
1. Make a weather scrapbook. Use the magazines for pictures.
2. Find pictures of different kinds of weather. Try to find pictures of places that have weather similar to your city's weather. Find other pictures of places with different weather.
3. Glue the pictures onto the writing paper.
4. Under each picture in your book, write a description of the weather in that picture.
5. Make a cover for your book.
6. Bind your book and cover.
7. Decorate your cover.

**Extension II:**                                        **Weather**
1. Go to the library (take a library pass) and research how a weather analyst predicts the weather or read the books in the basket.
2. Predict the weather for the next five days in your city.
3. Use the Weather Station Worksheets (5) in the basket.

**Thinking Levels:**  Analysis, Synthesis, Evaluation

**Skills:**

- Demonstrates understanding of the concept of weather
- Distinguishes differences
- Compares, summarizes, and evaluates information
- Predicts and infers outcomes
- Exercises research skills

# Weather

**Read the current weather report in the basket.**

1.  What is the highest temperature supposed to be today? _____

2.  What is the lowest temperature supposed to be today? _____

3.  What season is it now? _____
    _____

4.  How will the weather change in the next month? _____
    _____

5.  How will it change in the next four months? _____
    _____

# Weather Station

**Day 1**

**Date:** _____    **Observer:** _____

**Weather Today:** _____    **Weather Prediction for Tomorrow:**

_____        _____

_____        _____

_____        _____

_____        _____

_____        _____

**Temperature:** _____    **Tomorrow's Weather is:** _____

_____        _____

_____

**Rain/Snowfall:** _____

**Wind Direction:** _____

**Barometric Pressure:** _____

**Cloud Conditions:** _____

_____

**Paste Weather Map Here**

# Weather Station

**Day 2**

Date: _____     Observer: _____

Weather Today: _____     Weather Prediction for Tomorrow:

_____                  _____

_____                   _____

_____                   _____

_____                   _____

_____                   _____

Temperature: _____     Tomorrow's Weather is: _____

_____                   _____

_____

Rain/Snowfall: _____

Wind Direction: _____

Barometric Pressure: _____

Cloud Conditions: _____

_____

**Paste Weather Map Here**

# Weather Station

**Day 3**

Date: _____     Observer: _____

Weather Today: _____     Weather Prediction for Tomorrow:

_____     _____

_____     _____

_____     _____

_____     _____

_____

Temperature: _____     Tomorrow's Weather is: _____

_____     _____

_____

Rain/Snowfall: _____

Wind Direction: _____

Barometric Pressure: _____

Cloud Conditions: _____

_____

**Paste Weather Map Here**

# Weather Station

**Day 4**

Date: _____    Observer: _____

Weather Today: _____    **Weather Prediction for Tomorrow:**

_____    _____

_____    _____

_____    _____

_____    _____

_____    _____

Temperature: _____    Tomorrow's Weather is: _____

_____    _____

Rain/Snowfall: _____    _____

Wind Direction: _____

Barometric Pressure: _____

Cloud Conditions: _____

_____

**Paste Weather Map Here**

# Weather Station

**Day 5**

Date: _____     Observer: _____

Weather Today: _____     Weather Prediction for Tomorrow:

_____     _____

_____     _____

_____     _____

_____     _____

_____

Temperature: _____     Tomorrow's Weather is: _____

_____     _____

Rain/Snowfall: _____     _____

Wind Direction: _____

Barometric Pressure: _____

Cloud Conditions:_____

_____

**Paste Weather Map Here**

# Phase II–Creative Teaching: Small-Group Activities

Now that the students have had time to explore a variety of content materials at the basket center, you will begin to notice that some children have a keen interest in specific subjects. They will want to investigate further and will need someone with expertise in that field to guide them. Part II deals with the organization of small-group activities and suggestions for student participation and creative works from the areas of art, calligraphy, drama, food and nutrition, foreign languages, music, reading, science, and writing.

"We know what we are,
but not what we may be."

—William Shakespeare

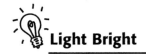 

## Volunteer Teachers

Reviewing your Parent/Community master list, you should have already identified volunteer teachers for small-group teaching. You may have to give them ideas for student creations, but the content of the materials and the way they teach content is up to them, hence the title *Creative Teaching*. Teachers will welcome the freedom from creating lesson plans on subjects they may know little about.

All Creative Teaching lessons occur at Light Bright. These lessons are scheduled during the last hour of the school day to avoid conflicting with the morning basket exploration. Inform your volunteer teachers that their lessons should last about an hour, including clean-up time.

Scheduling is important, and your volunteer coordinator is in charge. You may not have enough volunteer teachers to teach every day. You need to determine if you will have to repeat lessons. If so, it can be arranged that the volunteer teaching a specific lesson be scheduled to teach the same lesson twice in a given week. If you decide that it is not necessarily important that your gifted students be exposed to all Creative Teaching lessons, then your scheduling is more flexible.

You will have to establish with the volunteer teachers the number of students they feel comfortable teaching. It is recommended that no more than 10 students be in a small group at a given time.

In addition to actually teaching content to small groups, consider bringing in guest speakers from various occupations to share information about their professions. Note any child who appears to be very interested in a particular presentation—these students are good candidates for mentorship in Phase III.

## Schedules

### Classroom Model

Determining which students go to which small-group activity can be arranged in several ways. Student participation can be based on interest or talent, rotating schedules, or random selection. There are no formal requirements for students to take part in Creative Teaching lessons.

You do not need to be a trained teacher to know when a child is very interested in or has a special talent in science, art, mathematics, computers, and so forth. Thus, when a volunteer is scheduled to teach a science lesson, those students especially interested in science would participate. Those who have a talent in music or art would participate in those lessons, and so on.

You may want to set up a rotating schedule, much like some teachers do with their reading groups and activity centers. For example, you have three reading groups:

- Foxes (high—probably contains most of your gifted students)
- Birds (average)
- Tigers (below average)

While the Foxes are at a Creative Teaching group at the Light Bright Center, the Birds could be working on an assignment and the Tigers could be involved in a lesson with the classroom teacher.

The next time a volunteer teacher comes in, the Birds could go to the Light Bright Center for Creative Teaching, the Tigers could work on an assignment, and the Foxes could be doing a lesson or creative problem solving with the classroom teacher. Or, they could work on individual projects such as research at the library or carry over projects from the Light Bright Basket Center. You could also coordinate Kids Teaching Day with Creative Teaching lessons, that is, having both occur at the same time.

If other grade-level teachers are sending students to Creative Teaching at the same time, you probably will not be able to send all of your Foxes. Again, you may have to schedule the same Creative Teaching lesson more than once if you feel that all of the Foxes or more children should be exposed to the lesson. Depending on your student population, you may opt to have students attend by classrooms. Mrs. Jones' group goes every Tuesday, Mr. Smith's group goes every Wednesday, and so on. Rotating schedules will provide more work for the classroom teacher, as well as the volunteer coordinator, and this must be taken into consideration.

Random selection seems to be the most flexible method of sending children to Creative Teaching. It is 12:45 p.m. and you know that a volunteer teacher is coming at 1 p.m. to teach a lesson. You look around your classroom and notice that many students are occupied with what they are doing, some have unfinished work, some are going to special classes, and so forth. That will probably leave a few with nothing to do. As these are more than likely some of your gifted students, they are the ones selected to go to Creative Teaching.

At other times, you will notice that Mrs. Jones is doing a special project with her class and needs to have all students present. This allows other teachers to send more than their usual share of children. In appreciation for the volunteer's time, you should make sure that the number of students your volunteer requested to teach be present.

On some occasions, when you know a volunteer is coming in to teach or a guest speaker is arriving in 15 minutes, simply ask the class who would like to go. Usually, only the children who are really interested will raise their hands. If there are too many who want to go, then it is up to the individual teacher to select. You might say that random selection is a spur-of-the-moment decision after assessing the classroom at the time. This method allows the teacher to control who goes when. If a special project is going on in the classroom, teachers are not bound to schedules.

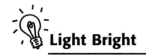 

## Pull-Out Model

As the gifted specialist, you could opt to have all three phases of Light Bright occurring at the same time. This depends upon the size of your resource center. It is easily manageable to have one group of children exploring baskets with one or two volunteers, one group in a Creative Teaching lesson, and one group in a lesson with you or working on individual projects. Several children could be visiting occupational sites or participating in a mentorship activity. When guest speakers are present, all students should participate.

If your resource center is small, you could arrange your schedule much like the Classroom Model. Or, you could have basket exploration and mentorship in the morning, Creative Teaching and guest speakers in the afternoon. Of course, much of this will depend on when the volunteers can give their time. Your volunteers deserve first consideration.

## Resource Notebook

It is recommended that teachers begin a Light Bright Resource Notebook containing the names of resource parents and community members, addresses, phone numbers, e-mail, occupations, talents, interests, hobbies, and days and times available. You will get this information from your Parent/Community master list. Your notebook should be alphabetized according to subject and could be color-coded according to subject—a great job for the Volunteer Coordinator.

The activities presented here came from our Resource Notebook. They are not exhaustive, and your topics may end up quite different depending on resources available to you.

Following is a page for your Resource Notebook and for volunteer teachers in Phase II. It is designed for you to copy and use as a title page in your notebook. Another page is included for you to make a list of possible guest speakers.

The following Phase II forms are designed for you to complete information on *your* resource persons. Certain sections on the remaining pages intentionally have not been completed so that you may fill in names, addresses, and so forth of volunteer teachers from your own community and insert in your notebook.

A blank form concludes this section, as you may come up with new Phase II ideas to insert in your Resource Notebook.

Once you've established that a parent or community member has a special talent, interest, hobby, or trade that it is appropriate to share with your students, they may need suggestions for possible student activities and products. Ones that have worked well at Light Bright Centers follow.

Many times, the volunteer teachers will already have lesson plans and ideas for products, and the only requisite for the teacher is to provide requested materials. A few such sample lessons are included for your consideration. They have been developed by Light Bright volunteer teachers.

## Appreciation

Your volunteers are an invaluable resource to the Light Bright program. There are many ways to show appreciation—at the very least, a thank-you note from every child who participated at Light Bright. Or, how about the idea of Volunteer Celebration Day? As a Light Bright project, the students are in charge of organizing a party for the volunteers. The party could include skits, decorations, refreshments, thank-you posters, and special recognition awards. Some students could talk about their most memorable Light Bright experience of the year. However, you choose to do it, it is essential that you recognize these wonderful volunteers for their effort, time, and dedication to children.

# Light Bright
# Resource Notebook:
# Volunteer Teachers

# Light Bright Resource Notebook
## Volunteer Teachers

## Sources for Volunteer Teachers

- Churches
- Colleges or universities
- Extension offices
- Fine art galleries
- Hospitals
- Interest/hobby groups
- Libraries
- Museums
- Newspaper articles
- Parents
- Public relation departments
- Retired senior volunteers
- Service clubs
- Teachers
- Zoos
- Professions
- Trades

## Your Community Listings

- _____
- _____
- _____
- _____
- _____
- _____
- _____
- _____
- _____

# Light Bright Resource Notebook: Guest Speakers

# Light Bright Resource Notebook
## Guest Speakers

## Ideas for Guest Speakers

- Audubon society
- Camera club
- Chamber of commerce
- Community concert association
- Community film society
- Computer club
- Exchange club
- Garden club
- Kiwanis club
- Lions club
- Rotary club
- Soroptimist club
- Symphony
- Theater associations
- Professions
- Trades

## Your Community Listings

- _____

- _____

- _____

- _____

- _____

- _____

- _____

- _____

- _____

**Hear Ye!
Hear Ye!
It's An
Arts Festival!**

A spring Arts Festival is a wonderful way to display student products from Phase II or Phase III, as well as creations from basket activities. Imagine … parents and community members enter the school and are dazzled by displays of student artwork, puppet shows, musical accompaniments, skits, and plays. All has been organized by Light Bright students, including planning, advertising, decorating, arranging the exhibits, scheduling special events, and so forth.

Tag art objects for the festival all year long. These can be from basket activities, Phase II, or Phase III creations. Aim at a variety of artwork. Students may even assume the role of the artists they have studied. Incorporate science displays and experiments, robots, inventions, and models.

Keep an ear open for musical selections that would be particularly entertaining. Include singing, musical instruments, and dancing. Do you have students taking ballet, tap, or jazz? Create an area where dancers or gymnasts can perform.

Have Light Bright students create a stage for puppet shows, skits, and plays. Students who have written their own poetry can also use the stage. Involve your chefs with recipes that have been created from the cooking section and include foreign foods. Have students dress in costumes from other countries and serve food from these countries.

**Plays
Skits**

**Puppet
Shows**

**Art Display**

**Name:** _____

**Address:** _____

**Phone:** _____

**E-mail Address:** _____

**Occupation:** _____

**Talents:** Calligraphy _____

**Interests/Hobbies:** _____

**Days Available:** _____

**Times Available:** _____

**Possible Student Activities:** Learn the art of calligraphy step-by-step. (Purchase a set of calligraphy guides from your local stationery store.) Students can share calligraphy technique with others.

**Possible Student Products:** An illustrated poster with a proverb or saying printed in calligraphy. A poem, greeting card, advertisement, short essay, or labeling for displays. Display finished products on a bulletin board.

Roman: Always move pen downward or moving forward.

ALWAYS KEEP PEN AT
THIS ANGLE.
30°

abcdefghijkl
mnopqrstuvwxy
abcdefghijklmn
opqrstuvwxyz

ABCDEFGHIJ
KLMNOPQRS
TUVWXYZ&
1234567890

# Never look a gift horse in the mOuth.

**Example of calligraphy.**

Name: _____

Address: _____

Phone: _____

E-mail Address: _____

Occupation: _____

Talents: _____

Interests/Hobbies: Clay/Pottery _____

Days Available: _____

Times Available: _____

Possible Student Activities: Students can make a pottery item of their choice from start to finish. Access to a kiln is necessary.

Possible Student Products: Finished pottery item, display item in library, display case, or at the Arts Festival.

Name: _____

Address: _____

Phone: _____

E-mail Address: _____

Occupation: _____

Talents: Art _____

Interests/Hobbies: Collage _____

Days Available: _____

Times Available: _____

**Possible Student Activities:**  Learn the techniques of collage, montage, and assemblage.

**Possible Student Products:**  An aesthetic and innovative collage product. Display at library, in classroom, or at the Arts Festival.

**Creative Teaching: Art—Commercial Artist**

**Name:** _____

**Address:** _____

**Phone:** _____

**E-mail Address:** _____

**Occupation:** _____

**Talents:** Art _____

**Interests/Hobbies:** Commercial Artist _____

**Days Available:** _____

**Times Available:** _____

**Possible Student Activities:**   Create a new cereal box design and product. Have students wrap old cereal boxes with blank paper, create a letter design for name, product symbol, or cartoon for front. List ingredients and nutritional value on back, create a recipe for back, put name of cereal company on box. Create an original advertisement for a product. Design an advertising poster.

**Possible Student Products:**   Completed cereal box. Any other kind of advertising for clothes, toys, cars, vacation places, and so forth. Post around school.

**Name:** _____

**Address:** _____

**Phone:** _____

**E-mail Address:** _____

**Occupation:** _____

**Talents:** Drawing/Painting _____

**Interests/Hobbies:** _____

**Days Available:** _____

**Times Available:** _____

**Possible Student Activities:**   Drawing techniques, painting techniques, map making, fashion design.

**Possible Student Products:**   Paintings, drawings, book covers, maps (illuminated or salt-flour), an art display in the library or at the Arts Festival, a fashion show using paper dolls.

**Name:** _____

**Address:** _____

**Phone:** _____

**E-mail Address:** _____

**Occupation:** _____

**Talents:** Fabric Art _____

**Interests/Hobbies:** _____

**Days Available:** _____

**Times Available:** _____

**Possible Student Activities:**   Students can create works of art using textiles, stitchery, applique, textile painting, banners, tie dye, and batik.

**Possible Student Products:**   Any samples of the above techniques. Display at Arts Festival.

**Name:** _____

**Address:** _____

**Phone:** _____

**E-mail Address:** _____

**Occupation:** Seamstress _____

**Talents:** Sewing _____

**Interests/Hobbies:** Fashion _____

**Days Available:** _____

**Times Available:** _____

**Possible Student Activities:**  Design fashions, draft patterns, study textiles, and sew patterns. Access to a sewing machine is necessary.

**Possible Student Products:**  A book of fashion designs, a sewing project, original patterns, a fashion show.

**Name:** _____

**Address:** _____

**Phone:** _____

**E-mail Address:** _____

**Occupation:** _____

**Talents:** Art _____

**Interests/Hobbies:** Lettering _____

**Days Available:** _____

**Times Available:** _____

**Possible Student Activities:** Basic hand lettering with pen and brush. Sign writing, layout and design for advertising posters, color application. Study of poster art, past and present.

**Possible Student Products:** Any samples of the above techniques, including posters. Students who participate could be in charge of advertising special school events all year or help advertise community events.

**Name:** _____

**Address:** _____

**Phone:** _____

**E-mail Address:** _____

**Occupation:** _____

**Talents:** Art _____

**Interests/Hobbies:** Printmaking _____

**Days Available:** _____

**Times Available:** _____

**Possible Student Activities:**    Linoleum cuts, silkscreening, and colorgraph. Study of printmaking tools. Woodcuts and etchings.

**Possible Student Products:**    Any samples of the above techniques. Display at Arts festival.

Name: _____

Address: _____

Phone: _____

E-mail Address: _____

Occupation: _____

Talents: Art _____

Interests/Hobbies: Sculpture _____

Days Available: _____

Times Available: _____

**Possible Student Activities:**  Students will learn the forming of three-dimensional designs using various materials such as clay, paper, wood, and plaster and the use of various tools.

**Possible Student Products:**  Any samples of above techniques. Display at Arts Festival.

**Name:** _____

**Address:** _____

**Phone:** _____

**E-mail Address:** _____

**Occupation:** Drama Students _____

**Talents:** Leadership _____

**Interests/Hobbies:** Drama _____

**Days Available:** _____

**Times Available:** _____

**Possible Student Activities:**    Have drama students help younger students create a play. Could be a puppet show, as well. Divide into small groups, each doing a separate play. Older students are in charge of script, directing, set design, make-up, costumes, and so forth. Younger students are actors.

**Possible Student Products:**    Final production of plays for school, parents, and community.

**Name:** _____

**Address:** _____

**Phone:** _____

**E-mail Address:** _____

**Occupation:** Drama Students _____

**Talents:** Leadership _____

**Interests/Hobbies:** Directing Plays _____

**Days Available:** _____

**Times Available:** _____

**Possible Student Activities:**    Practice and perform a play. Older students are in charge of voice, lighting, set design, costumes, and make-up. Students are responsible for all of the play production including advertising. Write and perform an original play.

**Possible Student Products:**    Play production for the school, parents, and community.

**Name:** _____

**Address:** _____

**Phone:** _____

**E-mail Address:** _____

**Occupation:** _____

**Talents:** _____

**Interests/Hobbies:** Cooking, Travel _____

**Days Available:** _____

**Times Available:** _____

**Possible Student Activities:** Study and discuss the lifestyles of several different cultures—Mexico, France, Japan, or Germany. Show movies or slides. (A volunteer who has traveled would be great—check your Parent/Interest Surveys). Discuss customs and rituals. Bake recipes from countries studied. Recipes follow.

**Possible Student Products:** Foreign country food fair at Arts Festival, foreign country cookbook, display of foreign foods, bake sale.

# Mousse

**France**

OUI!

WHAT WE NEED →

1 pint whipping cream . . . . . . . . . .
⅓ cup powdered sugar. . . . . . . . . . . . . . . . .
⅛ teaspoon salt . . . . . .
2 teaspoons vanilla. . . . . . . . . . . . . . . . . . . . . .

## What We Do:

1. Put cream into a quart bowl. Whip with egg beater until it will keep its shape. Do not beat it too much or you will make butter.
2. Stir sugar and salt into whipped cream.
3. Now add vanilla and stir.
4. Pour mixture into refrigerator tray and freeze for at least 8 hours. Makes about 1 quart.

# Pan de Muertos (Bread of the Dead)

**Mexico**

## What We Need:

¼ cup milk . . . . . . . . . . . . . . . . . . . . . . . . . . . . . . . . . . . .

¼ cup butter . . . . . . . . . . . . . . . . . . . . . . . . . . . . . .

¼ cup sugar . . . . . . . . . . . . . . . . . . . . . . . . . . . . . .

½ teaspoons salt . . . . . . . . . . . . . . . . . . . . . . . . . . .

1 package dry yeast . . . . . . . . . . . . . . . . . . . . . . .

¼ cup warm water . . . . . . . . . . . . . . . . . . . . . . . . . .

2 eggs . . . . . . . . . . . . . . . . . . . . . . . . . . . .

3 cups flour, unsifted . . . . . . . . . . . . . . . . . . .

¼ teaspoon ground cinnamon . . . . . . . . . . . . . . . . . . . . . .

2 teaspoons sugar . . . . . . . . . . .

butter . . . . . . . . . . . . . . . . . . . . . . . . . .

## What We Do:

1. Heat oven to 350°.
2. Bring milk to scalding, remove from heat and stir in butter, ¼ cup sugar, and salt. Let cool.
3. In a mixer bowl, combine yeast and water. Let stand about 5 minutes, then add milk mixture.
4. Separate 1 egg. Add yolk to yeast mixture. Save the white. Add remaining egg and 2⅓ cup flour. Blend well.
5. Divide dough into 3 equal parts. Shape each into a rope about 12 inches long. Braid ropes together pressing ends securely. Place on a greased baking sheet and join ends to form a wreath.
6. Cover and let rise in a warm place for 30 minutes. Brush with egg white.
7. Mix cinnamon and 2 teaspoons sugar and sprinkle on wreath.
8. Bake 35 minutes. Serve warm, cut into wedges with butter.

# Piñatas
## Mexico

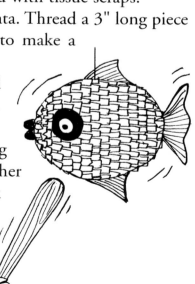

**What you need:**

- Large, round balloon
- Newspaper
- Scissors
- Glue
- Large tub
- Nail
- String
- Candies and little prizes
- Tempera paints and paint brushes
- Colored tissue paper scraps
- Blindfold
- Broomstick or plastic bat

**To Make:**

1. Blow up a large, round balloon and tie the end.
2. Cut newspaper into 1½" x 6" inch strips.
3. Mix one quart glue and about two parts water in a large tub until soupy.
4. Dip newspaper strips into glue mixture until wet and wrap around the balloon, wiping any excess paste off with your fingers. Apply three layers of strips. Let dry four days.
5. When dry, the piñata may be painted and decorated with tissue scraps.
6. With a nail, poke two holes near the top of the piñata. Thread a 3" long piece of string through the two holes and tie together to make a hanger for the piñata.
7. Cut a 3" section from the center of the piñata. Fill with candies and prizes. Tape the cut-out section in place.
8. Have the children make a circle around the hung piñata. Blindfold each child in turn and give him or her a broomstick. Each child has three swings to break open the piñata.
9. When the piñata is broken, all the children scramble for the candies and prizes.

# Pretzels

## Germany

**What you need:**

1 package dry yeast. . . . . . . . . . . . . . . . . . . . .
1½ cups milk. . . . . . . . . . . . . . . . . . . . . . . . . .
1 teaspoon salt. . . . . . . . . . . . . . . . . . . . . . . . . . . . .
¼ cup butter. . . . . . . . . . . . . . . . . . . . . . .
4 cups flour . . . . . . . . . . . . . . . . . . . . . . . . .

**What we do:**

1. Heat oven to 425°.
2. Mix in the salt, butter, and flour with the yeast mixture.
3. Knead the dough for 5 minutes.
4. Let the dough rise in a warm place for 30 minutes.
5. Take a portion (depending on how big you want your pretzels to be) and roll into a rope about 8 inches long. Shape into a pretzel and gently pinch ends together.
6. Sprinkle the pretzels with salt. Place on greased cookie sheet and bake 15 minutes or until golden brown.

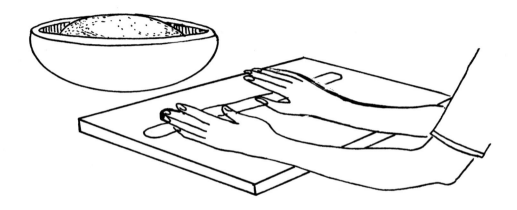

# Pilgrim Stew

**United States of America**

## What you need:

- 5 small potatoes, chopped and peeled
- 5 small tomatoes, cut into fourths
- 2 large onions, chopped
- 1 large can green beans
- 5 carrots, peeled and sliced
- 5 celery stalks, chopped
- 2 packages stew seasoning mix

## What we do:

Put all ingredients into a crock pot. Add 6 cups of water and 2 packages of stew seasoning mix. Turn to low and simmer for 12 hours. The average family would probably use half of this recipe. The above recipe serves small portions to a classroom of 20 students.

# Butter
## United States
## of America

Pour a large-sized carton of whipping cream into a a tall jar with a tight fitting lid. Shake and shake and shake. Watch the butter form. Pour off the buttermilk. Work and wash the butter. Pour it into a small bowl. Add salt to taste and serve on crackers.

# Toasted
# Pumpkin Seeds
## United States
## of America

Clean off the pulp of seeds but don't wash. Mix 2 cups seeds, 1½ table-spoons melted butter, and 1¼ teaspoon salt. Spread on cookie sheet. Bake 1½ hours at 250°. Turn every half hour.

# Sesame Seed
# Squares

**United States
of America**

## What you need:

½ cup honey . . . . . . . . . . . . . . . . . . . . . . . .

½ cup peanut butter . . . . . . . . . . . . . . . . . . . . .

1 cup powdered milk. . . . . . . . . . . . . . . . . . .

½ cup coconut. . . . . . . . . . . . . . . . . . . . . . . . . . .

1 cup sesame seeds . . . . . . . . . . . . . . . . . . .

## What we do:

Heat honey and peanut butter in saucepan. Add dry milk, coconut, then sesame seeds. Mix and put into a square pan. Refrigerate to set. Cut. May add nuts, raisins, chopped dates, and so on.

**Name:** _____

**Address:** _____

**Phone:** _____

**E-mail Address:** _____

**Occupation:** _____

**Talents:** _____

**Interests/Hobbies:** School Nurse/Nurse _____

**Days Available:** _____

**Times Available:** _____

**Possible Student Activities:**  Identify nutrients and their function in the body; discuss good health care and eating habits; research nutritional value of certain foods. Conduct research and collect data on a given group of students for a month—determine if nutritional intake is sufficient and recommend changes if necessary. Bake health foods from recipes. Invent health food recipes.

**Possible Student Products:**  Posters promoting good health care and recommended eating habits. Post around school. A kid's basket on health care or nutrition. A health food recipe book.

**Creative Teaching: Food—Organic**

Name: _____

Address: _____

Phone: _____

E-mail Address: _____

Occupation: Organic Cooking _____

Talents: _____

Interests/Hobbies: _____

Days Available: _____

Times Available: _____

**Possible Student Activities:**   Discuss food groups, processed food versus organic food, nutritional value of products such as peanut butter, whole wheat flour, home-baked bread, and so forth. Process grain into flour; bake organic food recipes. Interview people for their favorite organic recipes.

**Possible Student Products:**   Advertising posters for organic foods. Post around the school. An organic cookbook. An Organic Food Fair using only organic ingredients.

**Name:** _____

**Address:** _____

**Phone:** _____

**E-mail Address:** _____

**Occupation:** _____

**Talents:** Speak a Foreign Language _____

**Interests/Hobbies:** Foreign Travel _____

**Days Available:** _____

**Times Available:** _____

**Possible Student Activities:** Learn alphabet, numbers to 100, days of the week, months, family member names, manner words, songs, games, basic words, and simple sentences. Build vocabulary in successive sessions; study the country, lifestyles, government; show slides or films. Could incorporate foreign cooking recipes. Write letters to foreign students. Celebrate holidays in classroom as in a foreign country.

**Possible Student Products:** A booklet on country studied, including illustrations. A skit in a foreign language. Perform at Arts Festival. A kid's basket on a foreign country. A research report on a foreign country.

Name: _____

Address: _____

Phone: _____

E-mail Address: _____

Occupation: _____

Talents: <u>Piano Playing—Singing</u>_____

Interests/Hobbies: _____

Days Available: _____

Times Available: _____

**Possible Student Activities:**  Discuss voice technique, sing songs—include harmony and dance routines, create a choral production.

**Possible Student Products:**  Vocal production (concert) for school, parents, community. Could be a part of winter or spring concerts.

**Name:** _____

**Address:** _____

**Phone:** _____

**E-mail Address:** _____

**Occupation:** Teacher _____

**Talents:** _____

**Interests/Hobbies:** Trained in Junior Great Books _____

**Days Available:** _____

**Times Available:** _____

**Possible Student Activities:** Group discussions on selected books, critical reading skills. Share books with younger children. Write to authors, dramatize a part of a book, dress as a character in a book, and present part of the book from that character's point of view. Write a different ending for a book.

**Possible Student Products:** Posters promoting books to be displayed around the school. Puppet show on book, a radio and TV promotion for a book, a book jacket for a book. See other book sharing ideas in Chapter 5.

**Name:** _____

**Address:** _____

**Phone:** _____

**E-mail Address:** _____

**Occupation:** Fish Hatchery Manager _____

**Talents:** _____

**Interests/Hobbies:** Salmon Conservation _____

**Days Available:** _____

**Times Available:** _____

**Possible Student Activities:** Visit a fish hatchery, discuss the purpose of the hatchery, salmon cycle, types of salmon, salmon conservation, the effects of pollution on salmon. Research and complete reports on salmon and share with other classes—include diagrams, illustrations, and so forth. Raise baby salmon in an aquarium and chart growth, feeding, habits, and reactions.

**Possible Student Products:** Proposals to save the salmon, publish in the local newspaper. A kid's basket on salmon. A small model of a pollution solution machine to save the salmon from toxic waste materials; a booklet with illustrations that demonstrate the life cycle of salmon. Display at Science Fair.

**Name:** _____

**Address:** _____

**Phone:** _____

**E-mail Address:** _____

**Occupation:** Science Teacher _____

**Talents:** _____

**Interests/Hobbies:** Lab Experiments _____

**Days Available:** _____

**Times Available:** _____

**Possible Student Activities:**  Discuss the process of gathering, organizing, and classifying data, developing a hypotheses, testing the hypotheses, arriving at conclusions. Demonstrate methods of problem solving and inquiry investigation on any science subject.

**Possible Student Products:**  Science fair displaying student projects, models, inventions, reports, or experiments. An experiment for another class. Reports on famous scientists.

**Name:** _____

**Address:** _____

**Phone:** _____

**E-mail Address:** _____

**Occupation:** Marine Biologist _____

**Talents:** _____

**Interests/Hobbies:** Sea Life _____

**Days Available:** _____

**Times Available:** _____

**Possible Student Activities:** Describe what a marine biologist does, how data is gathered, how information is analyzed and classified; discuss environmental effects and pollution on marine life; demonstrate the kinds of experiments a marine biologist conducts. Show Jacques Cousteau films and Nova episodes; recommend solutions for environmental effects on sea life, classify sea life. Set up a sea life aquarium and record information on living habits, adaptations, and so forth; conduct experiments. Create journals using *National Geographic* for pictures—students fill in information.

**Possible Student Products:** A report on a sea creature; a sea life aquarium; a mosaic with shells and other items gathered from a salt water beach; original placemats for local seafood restaurants; a story from the point of view of a sea animal. A seafood cookbook, a kid's basket on sea life. Display items at a science fair.

**Name:** _____

**Address:** _____

**Phone:** _____

**E-mail Address:** _____

**Occupation:** Science Teacher/Taxidermist _____

**Talents:** _____

**Interests/Hobbies:** Taxidermy—especially birds _____

**Days Available:** _____

**Times Available:** _____

**Possible Student Activities:**     Learn and observe the process of taxidermy. Visit a museum. Lead a discussion about birds living in area, bird watching, and identification. Lead a discussion about bird habitats and adaptation to environment and harmful environmental effects. Discuss and recommend solutions for protecting birds. Write proposals to be published in local newspaper. Hear talks from Audubon Society.

**Possible Student Products:**     Dioramas of birds and habitats; paintings; diagrams, models, displays. Research report on birds, an original story from a stuffed animal's point of view, a kid's basket on bird life. Display at science fair.

**Name:** _____

**Address:** _____

**Phone:** _____

**E-mail Address:** _____

**Occupation:** Newspaper Columnist _____

**Talents:** _____

**Interests/Hobbies:** Writing _____

**Days Available:** _____

**Times Available:** _____

**Possible Student Activities:**   Tour the newspaper office, discuss the writing, editing, newspaper production process. Write and edit own articles, interview students, conduct surveys, and write summary. Write feature articles.

**Possible Student Products:**   School newsletter or newspaper, seasonal newsletter to parents and community.

**Name:** _____

**Address:** _____

**Phone:** _____

**E-mail Address:** _____

**Occupation:** Writer/Publisher _____

**Talents:** _____

**Interests/Hobbies:** Writing Short Stories _____

**Days Available:** _____

**Times Available:** _____

**Possible Student Activities:**   Teach the process of writing; discuss the elements of a good story; demonstrate illustrating a story, book binding, book covers. Share stories with the kindergarten class.

**Possible Student Products:**   An original book complete with illustrations, title, dedication, Could use word processor/computer.

**Name:** _____

**Address:** _____

**Phone:** _____

**E-mail Address:** _____

**Occupation:** _____

**Talents:** _____

**Interests/Hobbies:** _____

**Days Available:** _____

**Times Available:** _____

**Possible Student Activities:**




**Possible Student Products:**

# Phase III–Community Resources and Mentors: Individualized Teaching

## Mentors

One might say that mentorship is like an internship. Through mentorships, students can explore specific subjects of interest in greater depth than is possible in the classroom or even in small groups. Pairing a student with a mentor from the community who appreciates the student's talents can provide exciting experiences for both parties. First-hand experiences with the advice and assistance of an expert are valuable to the gifted and talented. Mentor experiences also provide excellent career exploration opportunities.

Besides pairing a student with a specialist, mentorship can also include on-site visitations and assistance to professionals, conducting interviews with professionals, attending seminars, and specialists serving as consultants to students on special projects. Going back to your Parent/Community Interest Survey, identify possible mentors and have your volunteer coordinator call upon individuals who have sufficient knowledge in the professional fields, as well as in the trades. Some of these experts will feel much more comfortable working with one or two students as opposed to groups of children.

Volunteer teachers from Phase II—Creative Teaching are other sources for mentors. From their small teaching groups, they will be able to identify those students who are highly interested or talented in their subject matter. Arrangements can then be made to teach those students one-on-one. High school students provide another source for mentorship. Besides sharing their talents and interests with younger students, high school students also gain valuable teaching and leadership experience.

> A nation nurtures
> what it values.
>
> —Plato

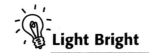 

Mentor pairing, on-site visitations, interviews, and seminars can occur any time during the day. The mentor's time must be taken into consideration first. The volunteer coordinator is in charge of arranging transportation and schedules. If the mentor is coming to the school, the time spent with students should not interfere with the morning or afternoon Light Bright hours. As mentorship occurs at Light Bright, they will need a quiet place to study. If the student is leaving the school grounds, permission slips, accountability, and food will have to be arranged. Light Bright volunteers and parents are very helpful in providing transportation to and from occupational sites.

## Conducting an Interview

Interviewing an expert in a field in which the student is particularly interested is a wonderful experience for the child. The Interview Form will aid children in preparing for an interview. They are responsible for contacts, interview questions, summarization of the interview, and a thank-you letter to the person interviewed. A Light Bright volunteer or parent should accompany the student on the interview.

## Community Resources

It is recommended that teachers add a mentor section to their Resource Notebook that includes the names, addresses, e-mail addresses, phone numbers, profession, trade or skill, days and times available, and topic of interest of resource persons in the community. The title page for mentors follows. Your mentor resources may end up different from the ones presented here, but these will give you ideas to get you started.

Although it is suggested in the following lesson plans that students visit occupational sites for first-hand experiences with professionals, it has become increasingly more difficult to arrange transportation. An alternative is to invite professionals to be guest speakers in the classroom. Many business leaders are recognizing more and more that business has a vested interest in improving basic and gifted education because its employees and managers are products of the educational process. Do not hesitate to extend an invitation to the business leaders in your community. You can find many active business leaders willing to help at the Service Clubs in your area.

# Conducting an Interview

## Interview Ideas and Suggestions

❑ Choose to interview a person who has a unique job or a job that seems interesting to you.

❑ Call and arrange an appointment with this person.
Date: _____
Time: _____
Name: _____
Address: _____
Job Title: _____

❑ List questions you would like to ask. Some examples are:
Why did you choose your job? _____
What do you like about your job? _____
What kind of training do you need for your job? _____
What is the best experience you've had in your profession? _____
_____

Your questions:
● _____
● _____
● _____
● _____

❑ Take your questions and writing paper with you on the interview.

❑ Interview the person. Write down the information you find out.

❑ Report to your class what you found out during the interview.

❑ What can I do next time to improve my interview? _____
_____

❑ Write a thank-you note to the person you interviewed.

# Light Bright Resource Notebook: Mentors

# Light Bright Resource Notebook
## Mentors

## Sources for Mentors

- Colleges or universities
- Fine art centers
- High school students
- Interest/hobby groups
- Newspaper articles
- Parents
- Research centers
- Small-group teachers (from Phase II)
- Teachers
- Trades

## Your Community Listings

- _____
- _____
- _____
- _____
- _____
- _____
- _____
- _____
- _____
- _____
- _____
- _____

**Name:** _____

**Address:** _____

**Phone:** _____

**E-mail Address:** _____

**Occupation:** Architect _____

**Talents:** _____

**Interests/Hobbies:** _____

**Days Available:** _____

**Times Available:** _____

**Possible Student Activities:**  Visit an architect's office. Observe the fundamentals of architectural drafting.

**Possible Student Products:**  A set of plans for a future domestic dwelling. A model city of the future with blueprints. Display at Arts Festival.

**Name:** _____

**Address:** _____

**Phone:** _____

**E-mail Address:** _____

**Occupation:** Banker _____

**Talents:** _____

**Interests/Hobbies:** _____

**Days Available:** _____

**Times Available:** _____

**Possible Student Activities:**   Tour the bank, observe the various employee roles. Study U.S. and foreign currency. Explain currency and the meaning of the symbols on currency to class.

**Possible Student Products:**   Coin collections. Reports to the class. A chart of countries and their basic unit of currency.

**Name:** _____

**Address:** _____

**Phone:** _____

**E-mail Address:** _____

**Occupation:** Computer Science/Computer Engineer _____

**Talents:** _____

**Interests/Hobbies:** _____

**Days Available:** _____

**Times Available:** _____

**Possible Student Activities:**   Programming techniques through VISUAL BASIC, an introductory program, or basic graphics program (younger students), 3-D imaging program (older students.)

**Possible Student Products:**   Cover design, original logo, original computer game—file in library for other students to check out.

**Name:** _____

**Address:** _____

**Phone:** _____

**E-mail Address:** _____

**Occupation:** Dentist _____

**Talents:** _____

**Interests/Hobbies:** _____

**Days Available:** _____

**Times Available:** _____

**Possible Student Activities:**   Visit the dentist's office and observe procedures, assist with cleaning tools, assist with X-rays, assist with dental hygiene. Put a baby tooth in soda pop and observe rapid decay.

**Possible Student Products:**   A report to class on dental hygiene, a diagram of teeth and explanation of decay to class, explanation of sample X-ray to class. A poster demonstrating good dental care.

**Name:** _____

**Address:** _____

**Phone:** _____

**E-mail Address:** _____

**Occupation:** Firefighter _____

**Talents:** _____

**Interests/Hobbies:** _____

**Days Available:** _____

**Times Available:** _____

**Possible Student Activities:** Visit fire station, discuss firefighter training, fire safety rules and equipment, and fire rescue techniques. Take a CPR course. Demonstrate CPR to other classes.

**Possible Student Products:** Posters for fire safety rules. Post around the school. A checklist for fire hazards in own home. Check for safety. A diagram of home or school including fire escapes.

**Name:** _____

**Address:** _____

**Phone:** _____

**E-mail Address:** _____

**Occupation:** Interior Designer _____

**Talents:** _____

**Interests/Hobbies:** _____

**Days Available:** _____

**Times Available:** _____

**Possible Student Activities:** Study design principles and elements of art; study colors. Assist with decorating a home. Design a room and furnishings—include color scheme. Build a model design of a room and furnishings. Make a color chart.

**Possible Student Products:** A room diorama—use a shoebox as walls, floor, and ceiling. Use wallpaper scraps and fabric scraps to decorate walls. Cut out windows and use fabric scraps for curtains, rugs, and so forth. Use matchboxes, empty thread spools, and so forth for furniture. Display at Arts Festival.

**Name:** _____

**Address:** _____

**Phone:** _____

**E-mail Address:** _____

**Occupation:** Attorney _____

**Talents:** _____

**Interests/Hobbies:** _____

**Days Available:** _____

**Times Available:** _____

**Possible Student Activities:** Visit an attorney's office. Visit the courthouse and observe a trial in session. Read about some classic trials; study legislature and Congress, how laws are made; criminal vs. civil cases; define legal terms. Visit your state capitol building. Your local YMCA may have suggestions for youth and government activities.

**Possible Student Products:** Mock trial including jury selection, judge, lawyer, prosecutor, defendant, court clerk, witnesses. An issue or a case debated and solved; a play of a case solved differently; a new law that solves a current problem.

**Name:** _____

**Address:** _____

**Phone:** _____

**E-mail Address:** _____

**Occupation:** General Physician _____

**Talents:** _____

**Interests/Hobbies:** _____

**Days Available:** _____

**Times Available:** _____

**Possible Student Activities:** Visit doctor's office, identify equipment, and observe and record a physical in progress or on self; assist with weighing and measuring; study the blood and the antibody system. Weigh and measure each child in class, record, and predict growth patterns.

**Possible Student Products:** Report on blood and types, including predictions of number of blood types in a given class; explanation of a physical to class; posters promoting good health care habits. Post around school.

**Name:** _____

**Address:** _____

**Phone:** _____

**E-mail Address:** _____

**Occupation:** Veterinarian _____

**Talents:** _____

**Interests/Hobbies:** _____

**Days Available:** _____

**Times Available:** _____

**Possible Student Activities:**  Visit the veterinarian's office and observe procedures for caring for sick or injured animals. Predict the future of the community's dog/cat population based on random sampling of information from neighborhood pet owners; use pictures of dogs/cats to write stories.

**Possible Student Products:**  A student-constructed survey to determine how many dogs/cats are neutered/not neutered in their neighborhood or community. Written proposals on pet control. Letters to the newspaper regarding pet control. A pet care booklet.

**Name:** _____

**Address:** _____

**Phone:** _____

**E-mail Address:** _____

**Occupation:** Pharmacist _____

**Talents:** _____

**Interests/Hobbies:** _____

**Days Available:** _____

**Times Available:** _____

**Possible Student Activities:**     Visit pharmacy and observe the preparation of prescriptions; discuss uses of drugs; discuss good/bad effects of drugs.

**Possible Student Products:**     An antidrug campaign, including posters around school. Display of how many drugs resemble candy; research report on a specific drug or cure.

**Name:** _____

**Address:** _____

**Phone:** _____

**E-mail Address:** _____

**Occupation:** Pilot _____

**Talents:** _____

**Interests/Hobbies:** Airplanes _____

**Days Available:** _____

**Times Available:** _____

**Possible Student Activities:** Visit aviation company; study aviation history; study construction of airplanes; discuss transportation of the future.

**Possible Student Products:** Airplane models; model flying contest; model of solar powered airplane; model of invention of future transportation. Diagram of the parts of an airplane. Display at science fair.

**Name:** _____

**Address:** _____

**Phone:** _____

**E-mail Address:** _____

**Occupation:** Carpenter/Builder _____

**Talents:** _____

**Interests/Hobbies:** _____

**Days Available:** _____

**Times Available:** _____

**Possible Student Activities:**   Assist a builder in building a home a few hours per week.

**Possible Student Products:**   A small model home; a model home of the future—possibly a solar-energy home. Younger children can design and make a gingerbread house. Display at Arts Festival.

Easy Gingerbread House

1.  Use graham crackers for walls and roof, decorated cookies for windows, chimney, and door.

2.  Attach pieces with confectioners' icing. In large bowl with electric mixer at high speed, beat whites of three large eggs with ½ teaspoon cream of tartar until foamy. Gradually beat in one 16 oz. package confectioners' sugar until stiff peaks form. Optional: add a few drops of food coloring for colored icing.

3.  Decorate by attaching various candies and cookies with icing.

4.  Set finished house on a piece of wood or cover cardboard with colored paper. Populate landscape with marshmallow people, decorated animal crackers, paper walkways, ponds, streams, trees, or figures cut from magazines and mounted on cardboard.

**Name:** _____

**Address:** _____

**Phone:** _____

**E-mail Address:** _____

**Occupation:** Electrician _____

**Talents:** _____

**Interests/Hobbies:** _____

**Days Available:** _____

**Times Available:** _____

**Possible Student Activities:**   Work with an electrician for a couple of hours per week. Could purchase an electronics kit and electrician provides consultation. Test and maintain electronic equipment and circuits.

**Possible Student Products:**   Model demonstrating circuits, telegram device, alarm, bell, and so forth. Build a robot or a homework machine with flashing eyes. Display at science fair.

**Name:** _____

**Address:** _____

**Phone:** _____

**E-mail Address:** _____

**Occupation:** Restaurant Management _____

**Talents:** _____

**Interests/Hobbies:** _____

**Days Available:** _____

**Times Available:** _____

**Possible Student Activities:**   Visit bakery or restaurant kitchen; study principles of safety and sanitation, food preparation, nutrition, and menu planning; proper serving techniques; production procedures. Assist if possible. Prepare and serve food products.

**Possible Student Products:**   Menu, a new recipe, a cookbook, a report on proper nutrition and requirements for age group.

**Name:** _____

**Address:** _____

**Phone:** _____

**E-mail Address:** _____

**Occupation:** Solar Energy Heating _____

**Talents:** _____

**Interests/Hobbies:** _____

**Days Available:** _____

**Times Available:** _____

**Possible Student Activities:**  Conduct experiments converting the sun's energy into solar power. Visit a solar-energy-powered home.

**Possible Student Products:**  Models of sunbeam communicator, solar-powered radio, solar energy storage conductors, sun-powered electronic circuits, solar-powered vehicles of the future. Diagram of solar-energy-powered home. Display at science fair.

**Name:** _____

**Address:** _____

**Phone:** _____

**E-mail Address:** _____

**Occupation:** Photographer _____

**Talents:** _____

**Interests/Hobbies:** Photography _____

**Days Available:** _____

**Times Available:** _____

**Possible Student Activities:**     Visit photo lab, learn how to operate camera, how to create a good photo, framing, the process of developing, and layout. Take and develop own photos. Assist with school pictures.

**Possible Student Products:**     An original story or play using old photos. A photo display in library or Arts Festival. A show using a series of pictures of historical sites in the community. Photographs illustrating a skill, a document, or an event. Display at Arts Festival.

**Name:** _____

**Address:** _____

**Phone:** _____

**E-mail Address:** _____

**Occupation:** Gifted Math Student _____

**Talents:** _____

**Interests/Hobbies:** Math _____

**Days Available:** _____

**Times Available:** _____

**Possible Student Activities:**     Work with variables in solving simple equations. Study rational number concepts and apply to solving basic equations and inequalities. Study real number concepts and apply to polynomials and to the solution of quadratic equations. Serve as a mentor on any math experiment or project.

**Name:** _____

**Address:** _____

**Phone:** _____

**E-mail Address:** _____

**Occupation:** Gifted Math/Science Student _____

**Talents:** _____

**Interests/Hobbies:** Math/Science _____

**Days Available:** _____

**Times Available:** _____

**Possible Student Activities:** Study aspects of chemistry as they relate to foods, medicines, minerals, and atmosphere. Study chemical structure, chemical bonding, energy effects, acids and bases, chemical reactions, and organic chemistry. Serve as a member on any science experiment or project.

**Name:** _____

**Address:** _____

**Phone:** _____

**E-mail Address:** _____

**Occupation:** Gifted Math Student _____

**Talents:** _____

**Interests/Hobbies:** Math _____

**Days Available:** _____

**Times Available:** _____

**Possible Student Activities:**    Study plane geometric figures of lines, angles, polygons, and circles Study real numbers and their properties. Study exponential and logarithmic functions. Serve as a mentor on any math experiment or project.

**Name:** _____

**Address:** _____

**Phone:** _____

**E-mail Address:** _____

**Occupation:** Gifted Science Student _____

**Talents:** _____

**Interests/Hobbies:** Science _____

**Days Available:** _____

**Times Available:** _____

**Possible Student Activities:** Study motion of objects, cars, and space travel. Study light and sound waves. Study atomic structure and space. Serve as a mentor on any science experiment or project.

Name: _____

Address: _____

Phone: _____

E-mail Address: _____

Occupation: _____

Talents: _____

Interests/Hobbies: _____

Days Available: _____

Times Available: _____

**Possible Student Activities:**

**Possible Student Products:**

# References

Bloom, B. S. (1956). *Taxonomy of educational objectives. Cognitive and affective domains.* New York: David McKay.

Johnston, S. (1977). *The fun with Tangrams kit.* New York: Dover.

Renzulli, J. S. (1977). *The enrichment triad model: A guide for developing defensible programs for the gifted.* Wethersfield, CT: Creative Learning Press.

Renzulli, J. S. (1978). What makes giftedness? Reexamining a definition. *Phi Delta Kappan, 84.*

Renzulli, J. S., & Reis, S. M. (1985). *The schoolwide enrichment model: A comprehensive plan for educational excellence.* Mansfield Center, CT: Creative Learning Press.

Seymour, S. (1987). *The paper airplane book.* New York: Penguin Books.

Treffinger, D. J. (1975). Teaching for self-directed learning: A priority for the gifted and talented. *Gifted Child Quarterly, 19,* 46–49.

United States Department of Education. (1993). *National excellence: A case for developing America's talent.* Washington DC: Office of Educational Research and Improvement.

# About the Author

Upon her graduation from the University of Washington, Joyce L. Martin, teacher, consultant, author, and publisher, began her career in 1977 as a teacher of kindergarten and second grade. Since then, she has been involved with gifted education in numerous ways.

Joyce served on the Sequim School District's Extended Learning committee for three years. She created a parent committee for student enrichment programs and served as a consultant on the topic of thinking skills. Her long-standing interest and involvement in education for the young gifted and talented includes presentations on enrichment activities and mentorship programs.

Joyce has been a presenter at many state and national gifted conferences during the past 10 years. She serves as a consultant on gifted programs for students in the elementary grades, is a part-time instructor at community colleges, and has developed after-school enrichment programs.

The never-ending quest for materials and methods to help children renew the spark of creativity, to challenge bright minds, and to instill an excitement for learning resulted in the development and implementation of the Light Bright program. Dr. Rena F. Subotnik of Hunter College, New York, served as a consultant and encouraged Joyce to publish Light Bright.

Joyce conducts workshops in conjunction with the Light Bright program and continues to research ideas and activities for Light Bright centers. Future plans include writing and publishing more books for teachers of the young gifted and talented.

Joyce lives in Reno, NV, with her husband.